Hardik S. Brahmbhatt's

Success Gyan Of Expediting Process And Constraints

"For Engineering procurement, construction and manufacturing professionals"

"Connect the Vision"™

Nexus Stories Publication

Bhārata

NEXUS STORIES PUBLICATION
Surat, Gujarat, India.

Title - Success Gyan Of Expediting Process and Constraints

First Published by Nexus Stories Publication 2022

ISBN # 978-93-91529-97-0

Publication
Nexus Stories Publication
Surat (Gujarat), Bhārata
https://nexus-stories. com
+91 87800 80718

From The Author

The Need of Writing This Reference Book Is Mainly Because, As an Expeditor, Myself working In an Industry since Last 15 Years, no Reference Material Or The Small Handbook Is Available In the Organization Or In the Market, Which Can Explain The Basics of An Expediting Process. Henceforth It Is My Small Effort to Materialize the Process in the Form of the Handbook, So Others Can Understand the Process and Can perform better with their Sense of Wisdom.

Index

❖ What Is Expediting and why do we need it? 5

❖ Chapter -1: Understanding need of Expediting, Pre-preparation of Expediting 7

❖ Chapter -3: Information Gathering, analysis, and Reporting 13

❖ Chapter -4: Type of Field Expediting and Resource Management. 21

❖ Chapter -5: Prioritization and 3E METHOD, Conflict Management 37

❖ Chapter -6: Supplier performance Monitoring 50

❖ Chapter -7: Onsite Reporting, and records management 65

❖ Chapter – 8: Desk Expediting 73

❖ Chapter-9: Logistics Coordination 93

What Is Expediting and why do we need it?

Expediting is a concept in purchasing and project management for securing the quality and timely delivery of goods and components.

The procurement department or an external expeditor controls the progress of manufacturing at the supplier concerning quality, packing, conformity with standards, and set timelines. Thus, the expeditor makes sure that the required goods arrive at the appointed date in the agreed quality at the agreed location.

The need for expediting comes largely from Engineering Procurement & construction business and organizations, where the entire gamut of activities needed to be performed for one project or one task. An Expeditor or Expedition agencies are the links between procurement and end-user, where procurement and end-user have agreed to meet pre-determined or dynamic deadlines/results.

An Expeditor or Expedition agencies are especially needed in large scale projects, for Example, in shipbuilding or when a refinery is being erected, because a delay caused by late delivery or inferior quality will increase expense and could lead to unsatisfied clients, thus the loss of a project or reputational damage. To save these unnecessary costs and minimize potential risks, the supplier and customer may agree on the use of an expeditor.

These are experts from companies specializing in this field who keep track of the deadlines, supervise progress on-site and check whether the components/deliveries are properly achieved After inspection or other quality assurance procedures, they notify the involved parties about their findings; if everything is as agreed as planned and documented, then activities such as Deliveries and commercial aspects of the order will proceed.

As the different levels of expediting require different skills, specialists, many third-party expeditors specialize in only one or several of these levels, while few offer expediting services on all levels.

Larger companies normally have their expeditors who can perform all levels. Or they hire third-party expeditors. We will explore the expediting techniques and much more when a task is assigned to an expeditor.

So, inside this guide, we will be focusing on effective and challenging expediting techniques and exploring more.

***

Chapter -1: Understanding need of Expediting, Pre-preparation of Expediting

It starts with Accessing the Information and preparation for planning and execution.

Because information is a weapon and needs to be processed carefully. Information about purchase order history, vendor performance document overview is crucial for expediting.

Processing the information has to be done very carefully, and requires attention and patience.

We are talking about three stages of processing the information

- **The data analysis (technical & commercial)**
- **The History and past performance**
- **Agreed Terms.**

Anyone who has been assigned to the expediting process/assignment needs to understand the basics of information and take ownership of the assignment.
Let's understand these steps with incidents.

- **The data analysis (technical & commercial)**

Purchaser Mr. X's Organization has just finalized the procurement of Engineering Products from Seller Mr. Y's organization and the contract has been finalized between them.

The contract has been signed and the expediting has been assigned to the expediter.

Now Mr. Z is the Expeditor of the Contract and assigned for expediting. Now Mr. Z has been told to start expediting. So, Mr. Z' has collected the data from the Purchaser and started the analysis.

Mr. Z has been doing the analysis and making his footnotes.

Footnotes for Mr. Z

- Reviewed the purchase order/contract has been duly signed by both parties.
- Contact no and the concerned person has been identified for the first meeting point.
- All technical Documents, specifications are approved and given to the seller for execution.
- Delivery Terms and Committed Date of delivery mentioned in Contract.
- Special Requirement of the contract has been identified; the Approved vendor/Supplier list has been mentioned in the Contract.

- **The History and past performance**

Mr. Z has reviewed the Performance and Delivery Schedule from past orders and learned that Mr. Y's Organization has been consistently behind the Delivery Schedule and still managed to win the contract.

❖ Mr. Z Has Reviewed the last 06 months of the Delivery Schedule of the Supplier and identified that the supplier has been delayed and no proper justification is recorded in the System.

- ❖ Mr. Z Has collected the Data and kept it for Reference since the delivery terms have been compromised.

- ❖ Mr. Z has learned that the Supplier has been penalized for not maintaining the certain quality standards and Parameters which was agreed in the contract. Mr. Z has collected the data for future Reference.

- **Agreed Terms.**

Mr. Z has reviewed the Contract and learned the Delivery Condition is the Ex-Works. This means All Cost of transportation has to be borne by the buyer.

- ❖ As per the Contract, Both Seller and buyer have been agreed to the procurement of Testing and certification services from an M/s ABC Certification.

- ❖ Seller Agreed on late Delivery Charges of 0.1 % of the order value per week. If delivery commitment has been failed by the seller.

- ❖ Seller and buyer are agreed to a Committed Delivery date of 60 days with Purchase order acceptance date.

It is important to review and analyze the Assignment before starting the expediting.

Now Mr. Z has reviewed the contract completely and can proceed with expediting.

Conclusion: Accessing the Situation and analytical approach before starting any expediting assignment is a very helpful and basic thing to do to understand the requirement of procurement and seller.

***

Chapter- 2: First Meeting Point and to start Expediting

In the last Chapter, we have seen the Preparation of Expediting, now we are exploring the way to Start Effective expediting.

There's a three-way of Expediting, A Field Expediting. A Desk Expediting and An Agency hired Expediting.

The most common expectation is the Field Expediting, As a Designated Expeditor is assigned for the job.

- **Starting the communication**

Now with all the Preparation, Expeditor can start the process of Expediting, First Crucial starting point of Expediting is communication. When an expeditor is about to start the expediting, he or she has to give a formal intimation to the seller, concerned person, and his or her seniors that you are designated expeditor and you coming for expediting the process, Most Commonly used intimation method is the Email. Almost every organization on the planet use Email, it is the modern-day fast communication of the 21st Century.

A Formal Email has to be sent by the expeditor contains, minimum but impactful words in professional language.

For Example

SUB: Mr. Z's Expediting Visit for Contract No: ABC-1386 Dtd 13-JUNE-2019

Mr. Y

Greeting for the day.

With Ref to the above Subject you have been awarded the Contract No: ABC-1386 Dtd 13-JUNE-2019 and Undersigned is the Assigned Expeditor for the contract.

I have planned to pay a visit to your office/works for the progress of our Contract on this 20-June-2019.

The agenda of expediting is attached herewith.

Pls, Confirm your Presence via Return Email.

Thanks & Regards
Mr. X.

While Writing an Email for Expediting visit, all higher-ups and piers must be communicated equally, since an expeditor is the eyes and ears of the buyer in the field.

Another Way of Communication for a planned visit is a phone call. Nowadays we are living in the 21st century where telecommunication infrastructures are very well established and more accurate. Just compare the scenario in the late '80s where Cellular was not even born and most of the communication is made through longer calls, faxes, and Letters.

Planning of expediting visits requires prior clear communication to concerned authorities for the clear goal of expediting and information exchange between buyer and seller.

- **Communication willingness**

Now in both ways of communication confirmation of meeting date & time is necessary as in some seller Representatives are not providing equal attention to an expeditor, that's why formal & written Confirmation of meeting is highly desirable because wasting of time is not a good virtue in the business itself. Also, formal & written Confirmation shows your expertise in expediting, because expediting is all about questions, information, and outputs. The moment you asked for confirmation of meeting your expediting has started. Keep this thing in mind as the moment you have asked questions and expect answers within a certain amount of time, an expediting has begun.

Now a certain question arises in the mind of the reader is this?

What if a formal confirmation is not given by the seller?

The answer is very simple- the moment you have been assigned as an expeditor, it's your Responsibility to get things in order, and you will not rest until you get your desirable answer/output.

You can take the help of your seniors in this case but I advise you to go on your own to get things done.

So, first, you have to fight your own battle.

Conclusion: Expediting is not just a late delivery warning, but it has an assurance approach with ease of communication between, an expeditor, the supplier, and Procurement.

***

Chapter -3: Information Gathering, analysis, and Reporting

Meeting with the seller, and discussion for order preparation and the fact check of claims and data is an important part of expediting.

When an Expediting process has begun, the most informal inputs are given and certain Questions arise from it. In expediting information answers always lead to another Question or query because expediting is iterative and continues a process that is going to be documented and processed with information and data on a daily, weekly basis or desirable periods.

Let's Understand in Very simple words.

Information is received

Information is analyzed

Analysis Reached in conclusion

Conclusion Leads to Acceptance
Acceptance leads to Execution.

This is an ideal Process of expediting. But if everything is ideal then why need an expediting?

In Reality, Expediting is a complex Process that needs constant attention and Evaluation. That's why it is a very important process that involves a very methodological and improvised approach at the same time.

Basic Of an Expediting

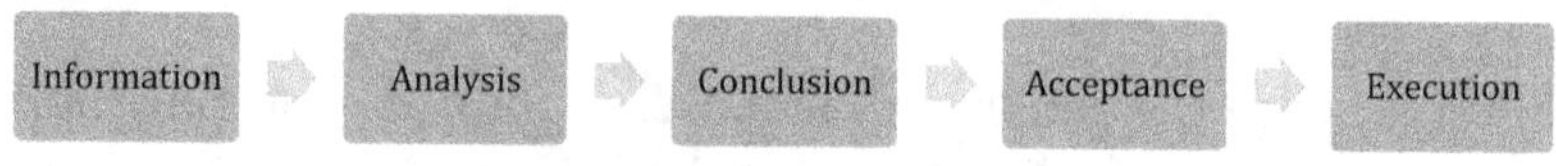

So, in the First meeting Information is everything, Information leads us to Questions and answers to the conclusion and Execution.

Information Gathering and analysis

Let's understand this with Real Case:

Mr. Z is a Designated Expeditor for a Small Water treatment Project. He has received an intimation to start Expediting for the project. While Reviewing the Data he has made Three Major observations that have not clear information either from the buyer or seller.

Observation:

1. After Carefully Reviewing Documentation and Data Mr. Smith Has found that in Documents no Specified Material of Construction is not mentioned for the Major 100 M3 Storage tank. This information has to be documented and approved.
2. While Reviewing Further Documents Mr. Smith has Found Some of the Components are being bought out directly from open markets. Where no approval for such components is being categorized in Category ABC Analysis. Which has to be done before manufacturing.

So, this is a very good example of being cautious. Generally, in our field, it is assumed that all formal Approval and documentation are being finalized before assigning to the Expeditor. Bur in field Expediting and business does not run on Assumption and Presumptions, it is fact-driven industry.

Mr. Z Has identified this observation and Reported and informed his buyer and Concern Department.

This Shows Information gathering and Analysis leads to Proactive, preventive steps.

Reporting

Reporting the key Steps for an expeditor. A Reporting to buyer, project Personals and Peers, gives a Real Picture of Field Progress.

Reporting methods and methods of progress update vary from organization to organization. Some Organization Preferred verbal inputs daily and some organizations preferred well-documented Progress Reports.

For Small and micro-manufacturing unit's daily discussions and updates are expected from Expeditor. When a large organization has an expediting Report, it is considered as a part of Daily Work in process updates as the majority of the project and procurement personnel rely on inputs from expeditors.

The report is materialized documentation of Discussion, henceforth Reporting is Important. Every organization has its way, methods, and Formats of Reporting. In Field, an Expeditor has to be prepared a Visit Report, Expediting Report, or another way of Reporting. In reporting the information has to be mentioned clearly. Reporting information has to be categorized and useful. Unnecessary information has to be avoided.

In Reporting, information has to be categorized into four Categories

1. Process status

   Process status is measurable steps that lead to expediting efforts to achieve final results. Process Status contains % of works completed as per planned Date, Schedule, Committed Delivery Dates, Process Status is major input when ''plan Vs Actual'' analysis has been done. Process status is output information of monitoring & controlling. Monitoring of processes is an expediting job. Process Status has to be updated not only for reporting but as a comparable unit concerning the planned schedule.

Classification of Information on Expediting Reports and its importance

Process Status	Deviation	Constraints & Impact analysis	Resolution / Action

2. Deviation

   When Process Status shows Delay in Process Execution higher than a planning Time frame. It will result in a delay in the overall time frame. The deviation is Delay Analysis when Process is not performed in a planned time frame. Deviation has to be taken care of before it leads to major constraints, so identifying the Reason for Deviation is the importance of expediting.

3. Constraints and impact analysis
   Constraint arises when a flow in the process has been ignored, foul play in following the Procedure, Delay in Resource allocation, and many other reasons can be when the constraint is found. And constraints arise unexpectedly even if all preventive measures have been taken. So, when constraints arise in expediting flow then it has to be notified, analyzed for impact analysis, and prioritized to be eliminated or resolved.

4. Resolution/ Action list.
   When a constraint arises in observation or runs expediting flow. It has to be addressed, prioritized, and to be resolved immediately. Why? When an expeditor does an impact analysis for constraint, it may result in a delay outside the planning/delivery time frame. This leads to extra time to complete a defined task when some or majority of your resources are engaged for some period which leads to rearranging the whole planning/delivery schedule. So to resolve a constraint it has to be addressed and prioritized firstly, so other resources and processes must not be affected, or list amount of delay can be insured, minimal cost and time can be provided for resolution.

   In addition, here Reporting Means it is not just to file a form or prepare a very lengthy and detailed analysis but to give your peers a clear picture. Where necessary protocols of on organization have to be followed.

   Henceforth we will study these four terms with a case study.

Process status

First of all, don't be overwhelmed with these words. Because knowingly unknowingly we use this technique in an Expediting every day. Mr. Z is a project expediter for a small water treatment project which includes pre-construction, fabrication, and installation activities. Mr. Z has started routine expediting for this project and he has observed a storage tank for process water is not being manufactured on time when it is supposed to be gone for manufacturing from 2 weeks after the order finalization. Mr. Z has asked the supplier about the status and demanded a reason for the delay.

The supplier has told Mr. Z that his storage tank is being manufactured at the sub-supplier location he has other priorities and he has not confirmed the order and has not started the manufacturing yet, supplier has started communication from his office but the results and efforts are not paid off and conditions are the same.

So, this is an example of the process status.

Deviation

When Mr. Z Identifies the Delay in the process and compares it with planned Dates. It is a deviation. In simpler words, our side planned Date or planning Schedule leads to the deviation. Likewise, this terminology is also used in the quality control process, but expediting Deviation is generally used for delays in the process. This Terminology is very different from one organization to another.

Constraints & impact analysis, Resolution/ **Action.**

Scenario-1

After Finding and acknowledging deviation in planning. Mr. Z has Addressed the deviation and to the supplier for not attempting and attending to the issue first hand. The supplier briefed him about the delay that from the Design point of view, the storage tank material of construction is not being finalized. Now it has been finalized, and the storage tank will be manufactured As per Reinforced Plastics, which is rust-resistant and lightweight material. Now After the new Development supplier can go for manufacturing within a week and overall 4 weeks delivery period will be achieved.

Scenario -2

Now I have changed the Scenario to understand from another angle.
When Mr. Z has found out that the Storage tank is manufacturing is 1 week behind the schedule. He has asked the supplier for the reason and made up a plan.

The supplier told Mr. Z that the storage tank is being manufactured at the sub-supplier location and the sub-supplier has not been given the priority due to his commitment to other customers and his manufacturing schedule is rigid and cannot be flexible till 04 weeks. Although suppliers have negotiated to the best level neither a positive outcome has been reached. Henceforth Mr. Z has to intervene. He has set up a meeting with the sub-supplier the next day.

Mr. Z has a meeting with the Sub supplier for the Speed up process and analysis purposes. Since Mr. Z Has explained that the storage tank is the crucial part and needs to be prepared with the project Schedule otherwise, late delivery and penalty charges, separate transportation expense, ideal manpower Reimbursement, and other worst impact can come ahead which is resulting in loss to both parties.

After a very excruciating Discussion and exploring the best way to prevent the constraint of Delay. Sub supplier has agreed to start manufacturing storage tank in extra shifts with added manpower to patch with the Project Schedule. Since Mr. Z has worked closely with the sub-supplier Manager to Review every possible outcome. All parties agreed to save time and cost and prepare the makeup plan.

Now in both cases, Expeditor has to follow the methodology of progress status, deviation, constraints and impact analysis, resolution/action list.

It may seem easy but it is an iterative Process till a Solution emerges from the situation. So the expeditor has to explore all worst-case scenarios and has to decide with mutual agreement.

On the final note, this kind of Situations must be Resolved and has to be updated to the procurement and concerned persons.

An Expeditor must report the constraint while a solution is being analyzed, and has to give the solution as well.

Conclusion: in the view of expediting, Information is a weapon of choice, which can be utilized for mostly constructive purposes, to prevent unnecessary delay.

***

Chapter -4: Type of Field Expediting and Resource Management.

Expediting is nowadays not just a late delivery warning; it has derived in different types of methods.

Further will understand the type of expediting needed or implied as per the situation and will understand resource management with an expediting point of view.

Expediting has been divided into Four Major categories.

1. Routine Status check
2. Exceptional expediting
3. Advance expediting
4. Replacement expediting.
5. Resident Expediting

Routine Status check

This Method is the very basic of Expediting and is commonly used by Procurement piers. In this method an expeditor can be assigned at the very beginning of the process or can be assigned in the middle of the process, to ensure timely delivery.

In routine status check involvement of an expeditor is very limited to the mile stone check, Daily updates, delivery verifications, daily visits as the risk of major constraints are very low. Henceforth expeditor inputs are milestone basis, engagement and focusing on the whole process may not be required. Ana expeditor involvement is needed when the milestone is behind as planned, the schedule is not being followed as planned. In this method, day-to-day expeditor involvement is desired till delivery.

Routine status check is also being used as a pressure technique where the supplier has fallen the delivery dates, and to monitor and control procurement pier will assign an expeditor to delay analysis and to ensure timely delivery. When an expeditor is in the shop, he/she can constantly monitor the process and follow up on a day-to-day basis.

Routine status check ensures that sufficient resources are being allocated to the process and in any condition, resources cannot be utilities for other purposes till delivery is completed.

For Example, M/s ABC Gear has an order of 10,000 no of gear components within 60 days of committed delivery. Since M/s ABC gear has provided manufacturing and delivery schedules.

A routine status check can be applied to ensure gear components are being manufactured and delivered as per the schedule.

M/s ABC Gear							
Order No: 13-1986							
Planed Delivery		Actual Delivery	Actual Delivery	Actual Delivery	Actual Delivery	Actual Delivery	Actual Delivery	Actual Delivery
Days	Planned Qty	Days 1-10	Days 11-20	Days 21-30	Days 31-40	Days 41-50	Days 51-60	Delay in Nos
1-10	1500	1500						0
11-20	1500		1500					0
21-30	1500			**800**				700
31-40	1500				1500			0
41-50	1500					**2800**		-1300
51-60	2500						1900	600
Total	10000							

Now As per the Schedule Every 10 Days Delivery is assured. As in for the first 20 days Delivery has been made as per the commitment. But between 21 to 30 Days half of the components Delivered against commitment, but after assigning the expeditor and delivery has been made up between 41 to 40 days, and overall commitment has remained valid and achieved.

Routine status check is a useful method to prevent shortfall deliveries and where very few follow-ups are required.

Exceptional Expediting

Exceptional Expediting As it is the name suggests, it is being used for highly critical and important items being added on a very tight and rigid schedule. Henceforth exceptional expediting is needed it is also called Fast Track expediting, Exceptional Expediting is a high pressure and stress type of expediting, when the original promise date is revised, to an earlier short period frame. Or when the original promised Date is missed by the supplier. This expediting has a more authoritative and demanding approach from procurement said because it has a revised delivery date, which suggests that things are not in order and has to make an exception in every area to achieve promised delivery.

For example, a small water treatment project has the delivery of 4 weeks when a client is requested to deliver within 3 weeks due to high load on his current water treatment system it is not enough to satisfy the demand, henceforth urgent is expected from both sides, procurement naan and the end-user. Where an expeditor has to work on intensive and deep root analysis for the makeup with the revised schedule, revise resource management plan, revised delivery plan and to above all convince the supplier and the suppliers for the urgency which involves very tough negotiation & pressure tactics. So, in the response to the unexpected urgency. An Expeditor has to make everything except for the planning manufacturing delivery and installation areas of the project. The most feared outcome of this Expediting is when the supplier is not ready to make an exception when the revised delivery date is proposed, where procurement is also being hustled by the end-user for the revised delivery schedule. Too much pressure on suppliers and the procurement is applied by the end-user or the client sometimes this pressure and stressful demand Lead to the termination of the contract for the cancellation of an order.

Exceptional expediting is a very demanding & stressful method so it has to be dealt with extreme care.

Advance Expediting

Advance expediting is the most time-consuming constant monitored type of expediting. It is a widely used method in engineering procurement and construction businesses instead of focusing on just let delivery warning this method is used to ensure timely supply before it is manufactured, in simple terms An expeditor/team has to work with supplier for his part of procurement scheduling monitoring and controlling, delivery, Engineering and covers all aspects. This method needs constant follow-up, monitoring, reporting constraints and resolution management, resource utilization, resource requirement, and allocation, advance extracting is generally consistent with a Team of expeditors/engineers who possess different kinds of expertise under one leadership.

Henceforth advance expediting use milestone, critical path method, scheduling, and other management techniques to identify critical steps at supplier manufacturing/production process. This is the dynamic type of process where multiple resources are being assigned and reassigned, allocated till delivery and execution is completed.

This expediting method reporting structure is more defined and involves a majority of Preventive and corrective actions. Advance expediting consistency of multi-discipline is being worked in a harmonious interconnected way where procurement is not being top of the program but is the authority of procurement is more linear with other disciplines.

Replacement Expediting

Replacement expediting can be applied when an expeditor/team is not being effective to overcome constraints related to delivery and behavior.

Replacement expediting can be done by a single person or can be performed through a team.

When the procurement pier decided to replace the existing expeditor/ team. It is not welcomed by the current expeditor/team. But the decision of replacement is the second last option left for the procurement, other than the amendment in the current committed delivery schedule. Replacement expediting is applied when the current expeditor/team is not being able to reach the committed set of parameters.

Replacement Expediting is not to be counted as a discredit to the team or individual. But sometimes another set of eyes reveals new information or another way to deal with the constraints more effectively.

As A Real Case Study, I am sharing my own Experience where Replacement Expediting is very supportive.

As Replacement Expediting, I have been Assigned to Resolve A Conflict of Non-availability of top housing of Degassed water storage tank (Refer Image), where top housing of tank was not manufactured due to non-availability of material, and the project is Delayed 04 weeks where the tank is Completed and ready to dispatch. Despite Several reminders from the project team, the Assigned Expeditor couldn't find material for top housing for manufacturing in-house workshop. Finally, the case was assigned to my Manager and he told me to get Resolve this issue immediately basis As the project was getting delayed and we couldn't serve our client on time and almost 04 weeks Delay was unbearable on both sides, hence I have Studied Full Drawing and requirement of Top housing, and it was 24" Diameter Housing which was needed for Gas treatment.

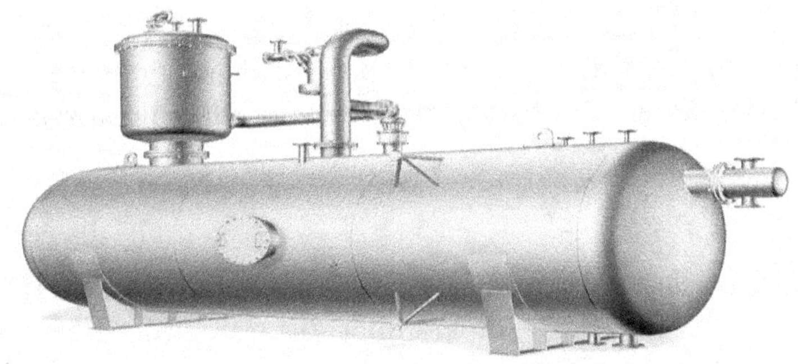

I had checked with my store department for material availability and they don't have a clear answer, as I have personally paid a visit for checking with the store. And upon asking the material they had checked their inventory and told me no material Available for Rolling of such small diameter housing and I have to generate a purchase demand note and get it from the purchasing department. Since it was delayed 04 weeks I had to improvise to overcome such a short notice solution, I had a Few moments of thinking and then I realized that the Diameter of top doom housing is 24" and we had a large stock of 24" Diameter Seamless pipes and we can use it for top housing, where top dish end was available and bottom flanges were available, we just have to get approval from client for change of material, I had immediately Asked my Manager for my proposal and approval of the client, within 01 hours, I got the approval from the client and we had proceeded for top housing manufacturing, whiten 06 hours top housing was completely manufactured, tested, inspected, painted and assembled, and very next day it was dispatched at client's location for installation.

It was very unique Experience for me and my manager, As very next day our efforts for quick resolution and actions were acknowledged and rewarded with appreciation from management and the project team, and in next upcoming days, we were part of the project team, where we have to show our other improvised and unique ideas, inputs to reach the common goal of service and completion of the project.

Resident Expediting.

Resident Expediting is a continuous type of expediting, where an Expeditor or number of expeditors work on different areas of requirement. At first glance, it feels like a more expensive step but it is the most beneficial type of expediting, where high stakes of businesses are involved. It requires expeditor to be deputed at the location of the supplier to maintain the delivery date very meticulously due to the high criticality nature of the items. Resident Expediting is preferred among other expediting methods where supplier performance analysis, daily monitoring and controlling, Daily Reporting, quality coordination, sub-supplier movement monitoring, and other aspects are to be followed on a collective basis. Resident Expediting duration is defined as per the urgency of the business, it can be a week or even months to perform and achieve to do so.

Resource Management.

Each type of expediting requires different types of resource management, generally, expeditor roll is not limited only to follow up, reporting, delay management, negotiations but also includes resources management. Where an expeditor has to intervene to save the day.

Resource management is only limited to utilizing existing resources but it is the management of the resources which involves the addition, upgrading, and acquiring new resources.

Expediting resource management has not been considered as resource utilization because people misunderstood the difference between utilization and Management.

In Reality, an expeditor may not be privileged with the executive authority for the resource management, but as is the designated focal point between procurement and supplier, An Expeditor has to deal with the resource-related issues and has to manage them with a team effort. In the field of behind the desk, the expeditor has to manage resources for maximum and timely delivery. Resource management is applied when the supplier is behind the schedule for not keeping up the pace with delivery priorities, henceforth resource management is needed.

In the Expediting- Resource management falls under the 4 major categories.

1. Existing Resource Management.
2. Upgrading of resources
3. Acquisition of resources/services
4. Collaboration and Outsourcing

Let's understand Each Resource Management category with an example of Mr. Z who is been working with a supplier for a water treatment project with the delivery period of 4 week

Existing Resource Management

After being assigned to the Water treatment, Mr. Z has been reviewing the current manpower allocated to the project by the supplier for manufacturing the major components like storage tanks, pipelines, skids, filters, and others. Mr. Z has reviewed that small team of 04 Skilled workers are skilled enough to perform the task, and their performance is in line with requirements for the project, While Reviewing daily works operations, Mr. Z has observed that a small team of 04 workers is struggling with pre- preparation activities of the manufacturing where there 30% daily time were spent on nonproductive and unskilled labor operation. Mr. Z has observed this and asked the team for additional support for no skills operation, they had agreed if some additional hands can help them in their daily preparation, which can deliver the products within 05 Days earlier than promised.

Mr. Z had a meeting with the supplier Production head for the situation awareness and eventually, he had agreed to facilitate 02 more semi-skilled persons to help the team of 04 workers, now a total of 06 people can do better.

Where in this Mr. Z has managed to utilize existing only 02 no of workers and saves the 05 working day time, which can be utilized in the successor processes.

Upgrading of Resources.

Upgrading the resources is the better part of resource management where upgrading the existing machinery or particular skill level in person is beneficial for a certain period, also benefits may continue in the future. It may include other perks such as cost optimization, time-saving & more.

Let's understand this by example

Mr. Z an expeditor of water treatment project, ministering manufacturing facility of supplier and after a few days of observation Mr. z found that 02 out of 06 electric arc welding machines are almost 06 years old and now it is depreciated to the service lives, and its high rate of power consumption and repeatedly breakdown happening and till the repair attended by a technician, no backup machines are available during the repair and manpower seats ideal or allocated to other jobs, in his project major components are manufactured through welding operations this kind of delay is not desirable. Mr. Z has suggested supplier production head and other authorities the addition of 01 electric arc welding machine and one mechanical orbital welding machine can improve their wedding operations where 01 electric arc welding machine can be used as regular backup and 01 mechanical orbital welding machine can be utilized for special circular 360 Degree welding operation which saves manual labor and improving production by 30%. After a couple of more meetings and suggestions from the Procurement pier, the supplier has agreed to invest in up-gradation which is immediately beneficial to Mr. Z's project and it is beneficial to the supplier for upcoming projects.

upgrading means the skill set of employees has to be elevated to the next level to also fall under resource management, as in manufacturing techniques and Technology is expanding and evolving day by day, skill up-gradation of employee is the best way to keep up with the trends, for example as tin to operate of mechanical 360 Degree orbital welding machines required a certain skill set, where proper training an employee is a requirement of skill upgradation.

Acquisition of resources/services.

As in expediting constant evaluation of process and progress is essential for the delivery and successful execution, where there are a higher number of processes involved in the manufacturing. Overlapping overutilization and Fast-tracking of production, manufacturing and related processes will be followed,

Where over utilization of resources may lead to hiring chances, failures, to prevent the delay or failure, acquisition of new resources. Services are required. It may not be permanent but for a temporary phase of time new service/resources are procured.

In this acquisition of resources, and expeditor may or may be privileged with executive authority but his finding and suggestion are equally important to the procurement pier, where some time higher authorities are expected to provide solid inputs from the field, where the current situation is monitored by their workmate.

For example, where major water project treatment components are finished and sent up to the different units for finishing and painting which leads to 1,5 weeks in total, where in house finishing and painting facilities, can save time and can be done in 04 days, or A contractor can do this job in after factory hours on pro-rata basis in 03 days, where an expeditor has to give all options and inputs the procurement pier and supplier to reach a common goal for the specific reason to achieve timely delivery.

Collaboration and Outsourcing

In Expediting Collaboration and outsourcing has their way of doing it. Collaboration is the process of two or more people, entities, or organizations working together to complete a task or achieve a goal. With ref to expediting collaboration is considered as in to develop a sense between supplier's network, resources, and employees to achieve a final goal.

In this real world of capitalism, suppliers, sub-suppliers, manufacturers, process houses, small businesses, are connected and depend on each other. Henceforth to develop a sense of collaboration among them is necessary when things are not moving as planned. When businesses are operating with other local suppliers, sometimes a comfort zone of co-existence leads to overlooking the schedule and missing deadlines is the outcome expected. Likewise, suppliers' internal departments like production, quality, logistics, and other operational units and their employees also fall for the comfort zone trap where motivation needs to be applied through soft core or hard-core methods.

Henceforth Collaboration in expediting makes sense and sense among the resources has to be developed for the benefits of timely delivery.

It may sound contradictory Reference to resource management but outsourcing is also a part of management.

Outsourcing is the business practice of hiring a party outside a company to perform services and create goods that traditionally were performed in-house by the company's employees and staff. Outsourcing is a practice usually undertaken by companies as a cost-cutting measure.

As in expediting practice. In-house facilities of manufacturing are fully utilized and no further room left for added outputs than outsourcing can be helped to the system. An expeditor has to measure the utilization capabilities of suppliers to perform for such an initiative, where through meetings with suppliers and procurement decisions can be made for outsourcing. Where suppliers can be focused on primary core products and lesser important operations can be handled somewhere else.

Major reasons and needs for outsourcing are

1. Risk management
2. Cast saving
3. Space management
4. Improve quality
5. Cost restructuring
6. Focus on core business
7. Scalability
8. Time-saving measurement
9. Reduce Employee Engagement

Outsourcing may not be Relevant in some Cases, nevertheless, An Expeditor must have to think of the best and effective solutions for each situation.

We will refer to a case study when Outsourcing is preferred as the best option.

M/s XYZ Corporation's delivery is 30 days behind the committed delivery date it seems the supplier couldn't manage production on time after giving several late delivery warnings. To prevent more catastrophe an expedition has been assigned to the supplier.

While investigating expeditor reveals that that supplier has trouble to keep up production as per delivery date and demand, where his most time is utilized to supervise Manpower in daily operation activity. Material processing preparation and finishing activities, supplier himself has to monitor in-person production as his manpower is highly utilized and pending orders are rising, after very lengthy discussion & meetings. Supplier's late delivery reasons have been identified and addressed.

The top Reasons for late delivery are:

1. Supplier's direct engagement to manpower supervision and manufacturing operations. (lack of middle management)
2. Resources (machinery) are limited, no scope for the new addition of resources due to financial restrictions.
3. Supplier's time is invested too much in detailed daily supervision,
4. Absence of managerial Approach.
5. Lack of experience handling high-volume orders.

After assessment of the situation, the expediter has suggested utilizing machinery and tools by doubling up shift, where the supplier can hire an outside contractor who can utilize machinery and tools for another shift with his man power, so the supplier can focus on high priority item on 1st shift and less priority item can be manufactured in another shift, where outside contractor who can manage his manpower directly on the shop with the help of existing tools and machinery of the supplier, It is a Win-Win situation for supplied and contractor both because full utilization of machinery and tools has applied to double up production and lead time of 30 day is cut down by 10 days.

In this case, study full utilization of machinery and tools is the best option. As in practice, multiple solutions can be applied as per the expertise of the expeditor.

Conclusion: Expediting is a method of speeding up the process when needed, it also has an assuring approach to facilitate procurement needs. Expediting is not just a reminder, it has technical, commercial, and managerial skills combined in practice upon dynamic requirements.

***

Chapter -5: Prioritization and 3E METHOD, Conflict Management

An expeditor 's main function during the assignment is the Prioritization of the task as per a procurement's urgency or input from higher management. Setting priority is the crucial step as an expeditor has to directly intervene with the wonders management people as they have their priority schedule to follow when an expeditor has to manage the schedule with other customer's priorities and has to work closely with the manufacturer.

To facilitate procurement demand expeditor has to review the input, manufacturing schedule, plant date of the task, record management, inventory, vendor coordination, reporting, and other aspects of the manufacturing regularly. Since an expeditor may or may have direct access to the manufacturer's schedule and expeditor has to review the schedule and provide amendment/revision as per expediting needs. An expeditor to verify plan vs actual progress and process and has to expedite for the makeup plan activities after the delayed operation.

An Expeditor must have to review the manufacturing schedule provided by the supplier or he has to check the progress and process as per the planned /committed delivery date. In practice, not every supplier is providing manufacturing schedule to the procurement, instead of providing a manufacturing schedule, they provide their assurance of delivery through Email, discussion, and other verbal communication forms, As the procurement department has needed more than supplier's assurance of delivery, An expeditor's role is likely to be a negotiator for the procurement department in every scenario. Setting up priorities is a primary concern of the expeditor in every situation; hence expeditors have to rely on manufacturing plans, and other information, tools & techniques to establish a clean set of privatizations.

To set a priority an expeditor has to gather information from below mentioned tools,

1) Master production schedule
2) Material Requirement plan
3) Supplier's historical data
4) Procurement requirement analysis
5) Advanced planning and scheduling system

An Expeditor has to review the plan vs actual data to prevent delay and optimize delivery. Review of supplier's production schedule is mandatory because in today's world of capitalism no supplier depends on a single client for a single organization for earning the profits. A detailed analysis manufacturing schedule can reveal how much weightage is provided by supply against order/requirement. A review of the manufacturing schedule can reveal the information that the supplier is ready to commit to achieving the delivery date. A review of the manufacturing schedule also discloses the possibility of other customers' priority engagement, which is not important at the first sight but it has more impact on expediting priority. (We will discuss this in another chapter in a more elaborate way) An expeditor has a clear advantage being on-field or interacting with suppliers where an expeditor can sense/predict that supplier has other priority/ commitments to our customer's requirement.

This is an idle condition where we assume/presume that supplier is ready and will deliver as per the committed delivery date. In reality, the supplier is more focused on daily operation activities where he sees an expeditor as another promulgate authority. That's why expediting has been needed for delivery assurance and supervision.

In expediting prioritization, it has been crucial for the delivery, henceforth prioritization needs to be established, monitored, and improvised as per the situation, every organization has its technique of prioritization. Mostly applied prioritization techniques are described as under

1. ABC analysis
2. Ranking
3. Grouping
4. MOSCOW model Must
5. 3 p method

In practice, a well-managed organization can give a Priority plan to the expediter. While a functional organization or less privileged organization gives an expeditor to establish prioritization tasks who can establish prioritization plans and move the things as needed. In a real situation, expeditor must not be dependent on priority or requirement plan from procurement in such a situation an expeditor can establish the communication to the procurement/end-user for the required delivery plan.

Prioritization has many aspects but two main factors or key factors in the establishment of prioritization are financial management and requirement management. These are the key factors in the process of prioritization. In the field or behind the desk an expeditor has to work with a priority plan otherwise no clear goal of expediting serves a purpose. While trading and serving in the business an expeditor has to develop the ability to set a requirement plan with the interests of the procurement, end-user, stakeholders.

To understand Prioritization better there are three major defined types mentioned under.

1. Management Defined prioritization
2. Individual defined Prioritization
3. Improvise based prioritization

Management Defined prioritization

As defined in the name management defined prioritization is the most common form of prioritization as management has given priority to the items and explain to has to follow the inputs from the management defined prioritization provided

in some sort of format, instruction, the scope of supply, delivery plan, or as per the organization definition it could be non-verbal also management defined prioritization set of a clear requirement which is easy to target and helps to expeditor to focus in specific which items need to top priority. For example, management given a plan date of delivery is defined and gives clear instructions to follow on which an expeditor has to monitor the specific products/processes.

Individual defined Prioritization

This prioritization technique is useful and applied for small projects or small-scale organizations where the expediting scope is focused on the majority part of the item. As defined in this technique priority is been set by the assigned expeditor. This expediting is mostly based on the expertise of the expeditor where the expeditor has to discuss with the supplier to make a priority plan. Individually defined prioritization covers all areas of expediting from raw material management, manufacturing, delivery, site execution. Individually defined prioritization also helps to establish a single communication point between supplier and procurement as it helps the flow of communication easily from bottom to top without any additional reporting.

Individual base expediting is being used for the expertise of an expeditor where Procurement wants direct access to the manufacturing and wants to monitor progress closely.

Case Study: A small chemical manufacturing division needs a chemical mixing unit which consists of a pressure vessel, storage tank, piping, and other pumping items, where they want to complete delivery of the package within four weeks rather than focusing on individual item expediting the close focus on the delivery date where they want to package delivered at the premises and they will install the package with the help of their manpower.in this case, the part delivery is not preferred, henceforth individual-based prioritization is needed where part delivery, milestone-based expediting is not preferred. Where an expeditor has to work with suppliers to set up priority plans and has to monitor closely and report to higher-ups regularly.

Improvised Defined prioritization

Improvise prioritization is the technique applied when sudden demand for a specific product arrives and has to move this item ahead in manufacturing where no option is left but to improvise and adapt the new requirement. this technique involves a lot of debating, explaining, reviewing because both parties have agreed on a specific period for delivery which has to be moved to head and used to be monitored and answered on an immediate basis improvise priorities is known for jeopardizing other's well-planned operation and an expeditor to prepare the worst outcome. As improvised priority left a gap in the pre-defined priority plan. In which the entire manufacturing and planning schedule has to be rewritten, in a nick of time, or other operations must have to be dropped and needs only focus on urgent requirements and other planning is left unattended due to focusing on improvised demand. As in expediting improvised property left a gap on Successor or predecessor activities/products' manufacturing which impact has to be reviewed and the entire manufacturing schedule has to be rearranged.

For example, a Drinking water package consists of storage tanks, pressure vessels, filters interconnecting piping, pumps, control panel, membrane, and other components. Where a client demands a storage tank delivery on immediate business or within a week time due to existing storage tank operational due to corrosion and contamination. In which no further option is left but to give high priority for storage tank manufacturing. This kind of priority expediting involves a lot of awareness and working extra hours.

3E Method

To achieve desired prioritization, a successful communication method has to be followed, in expediting timely communication to the right authority is very important. To achieve timely delivery, a simple 3E communication method must be applied. Here 3E stands for

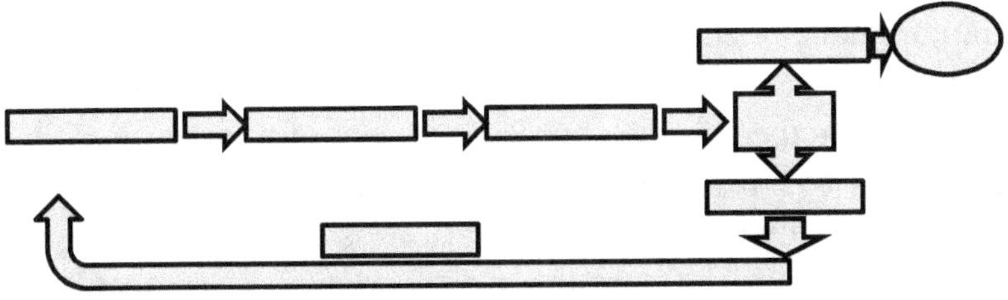

1. **Elaboration**
2. **Escalation**
3. **Execution**

Elaboration.

In Expediting elaboration is not limited to pointing out constraints and a requirement justification, expediting elaboration is more than a late delivery warning with its Ramification explained in a very effective manner. Elaboration of such a condition must have an authoritative manner. If delivery is delayed beyond 06 weeks, has a penalty of 1% of order valve per week, which is not a good business, and late delivery also hampered a site execution plan and also involves an unutilized man power for 02 weeks which is also a loss for procurement side and also from the supplier side. Henceforth late delivery is not expected from the supplier to maintain a good relationship and to avoid unnecessary conflicts.

Here the situation is perfectly explained with minimum but effective and statistical and fact-driven information which leads to suppliers thinking about the seriousness of the situation. Further elaboration of the situation must be acknowledged and documented in such cases where serious ramification is expected. Elaboration covers most aspects of non-compliance, non-corporation, neglecting of facts, ignoring order terms and conditions, contracts conflicts, management constraints, behavior analysis, deviation, requirement management, schedule management, and others. In expediting elaboration is part of managing skills presented by an individual. Here elaboration is part of an addressing mechanism. Elaboration is required in such situations when the supplier's performance is critical and needs to be maintained in a planned manner.

Escalation.

In expediting escalation is immediately followed by elaboration if the result is not achieved. Escalation is needed when a further elaboration of the situation is not honored or more hard steps are required, then for a stricter approach, escalation at the supplier's higher authority is needed. For example, when the supplier's shop floor manager is not giving priority to the planned schedule/committed date. Further, this act has been escalated to the general manager of production, who is immediately superior to the shop floor manager. In practice, many individual expeditors ignore the escalation step as they rely on supplier's feedback or action when in absence of such response, immediate report to the situation helps to recover on time which saves further expediting efforts. Escalation shows a more thoughtfulness, approach to the expediting which is expected in the field/behind the desk. As an expeditor individual must not hesitate to escalate the situation to the prompt authorities, even such a situation must be reported to procurement promptly as the expeditor is an extension to the procurement, and such steps are expected by the authorities to show ownership to the assignment. To escalate such a situation an expeditor must have to report the situation with given facts and figures, likewise, a process chart, plan vs actual, shows to support his view. Because a famous idiom shows: rather than describing 1000 words just put a picture to prove your view, henceforth an expeditor has to escalate a situation and also use a system, tools, and techniques for reporting.

As an individual, an expeditor has invested with the full authority from procurement to ask and challenge the facts for designated tasks.

Execution.

Expediting execution is not defined for the competition of particular activity, but it is also defined as expediting efforts paid off when such a situation is elaborated and escalated is being performed as it should be done as per the plan. Here execution means witnessing to completing a situation that is reported earlier through elaboration and escalation. No expediting is completed when such a situation is completed, reported, and witnessed.

Execution is the final step of expediting when such efforts are being paid off. For example delivery violation of 02 weeks has been elaborated and escalated through proper channels and now it has been completed in the 4th week. Execution must be endorsed and proven with facts, milestones, etc. Hereafter successful elaboration and escalation execution is generally the positive outcome of this 3e method. If a positive outcome is not achieved an individual has to repeat the process till the goal is achieved.

Conflict Management

In expediting processes conflicts are expected where an individual has to identify the conflict and has to exercise for resolution until you avoid it. In expediting conflict is majorly defined by,

1. **Priority Conflicts,**
2. **Financial Conflicts**
3. **Quality Conflicts**

Priority conflicts.

Priority conflict is the major conflict in expediting, where the supplier is agreed on earlier committed delivery date. And after revision in delivery is expected sooner than promised delivery date supplier is not agreed to deliver against the revised delivery date after much expediting efforts and prioritization exercise. It will become a priority conflict when the expeditor's deep involvement is not honored then it turns into a conflict where the expeditor's engagement is merely a pressure technique to keep suppliers at foot. When the supplier is neither read nor agrees to a revised delivery date. It is higher management's concern when after putting much effort in expediting nothing fruitful outcome is received. An expeditor has to set a keen eye on such interactions when efforts are not honored, in such a situation higher management intervention is the final option. Another form of priority conflict is when a customer has given a priority directly to the supplier for a required item, and the expeditor has also given a priority of another item from procurement. In such a case a due to lack of clear communication creates a conflict on priority requirements. As an expeditor, he/she has to review the source of priority before proceeding or expediting efforts.

Some Priority conflicts are not agreeable for both parties where no one is compromising on their terms and conditions, in such a situation a major outcome leads to cancellation/termination of contract/order. Since it is a business trade and expediting are the discipline of procurement an expeditor will or may not be witnessing such a situation.

Financial conflicts.

Finance is the major conflict in global trade that affects every organization on the planet. Even expediting such a situation comes when finance is a major conflict, where both parties agreed on delivery dates but due to some financial conflict's delivery couldn't be achieved. In such a situation an expeditor's involvement can be needed to know the basis from the procurement point of view. For example, a specific type of material is not available in the market and it has to be sourced from an overseas market, which involves additional processes like custom Clarence, import duty, government regulation, and restriction, in such process time is crucial and money is also a major factor for manufacturing special kind of product which involves a higher quality raw material and process, in which it is a time and cost consuming process where both parties have no option left but to substitute the requirement with lower standard category material. Which involves the research and development department, engineering department, where the expeditor's involvement is limited to a follow-up basis.

In major financial conflicts are reached to some degree of solution where both parties understand the gravity of the situation and reach a common goal for resolution. It may not be relevant to expediting but it is a knowledgeable experience where a more practicable approach is adapted by both parties.

Another financial conflict arises when the supplier is agreed on the revised delivery date of the order if the value is amended as per the given quote. It is a procurement step to honor revised quotes, where the expeditor can pass the information to the procurement, where his ability to address such issues is none. In general practice, such conditions can be encountered as it is part of the business. An expeditor has to know his limitation for the assignment and has to act on his fine sense of wisdom.

Quality conflicts.

Expediting quality is not an exclusive responsibility to the quality department but expeditors share some of the quality responsibilities, as he/she has direct access to the manufacturing from raw material movement, production, process, to final execution and delivery plan. In expediting quality conflict can be observed through visits, document review, test results, process evaluation, and other parameters that can reveal the conflict in quality. For example, during a visit, an expeditor has observed that a non-qualified worker is operating a highly sophisticated SAW (Submerged arc welding) machine where the quality of products may have compromised and been subjected to investigation and reporting. In such a case an expeditor has to submit findings to the supplier and procurement in a written manner, where corrective actions can be taken. It impacts the supplier that the expeditor is also aware of the situation, and it helps quality to be controlled and maintained. Where a keen eye on the situation prevents the major catastrophe ahead. Likewise, an approved supplier list can guide expeditors that no raw material or other material is procured outside other than the approved supplier list. Quality conflict covers a large no of points, where in this handbook I couldn't have addressed. Hence major quality conflicts can be prevented during expediting visits, in such a situation an expeditor must have some sort of quality knowledge that can be beneficial for the entire process.

Conclusion: Prioritization is key to Expediting, and an expeditor has to use his/her talent in communication to speed up the process.

***

Chapter -6: Supplier performance Monitoring

In a business trade, an expeditor encounters various engagements with the vendor, supplier, service providers, traders in which the expeditor has to make various meetings, communication, visits, and review of the schedule and other aspects of the expediting. In such a diversified discipline, multiple criteria are followed and observed on a routine basis. Which helps to monitor the performance of the individual, later this step helps to evaluate an individual. Henceforth keeping necessary data is important for the future. Because accurate data and correct information are crucial for any evolution.

In expediting expeditor has to contact and visit the vendor and supplier. Both are important for the business but there is a noticeable difference between vendor/supplier. In very simple words vendor is defined as:

Vendor: A vendor is an individual or entity, who sells goods and services for a price to the customers.

Supplier: Supplier is the one whose work is to provide the good or service required by the business.

In simpler terms vendor's engagement is limited in such cases till delivery of goods/services is provided. Where supplier's engagement is extended after delivery of goods/services is made. Just like after-sales services, supplier engagement continues in a more collaborative business way.

In Expediting Expeditor's responsibility is more focused and elaborated rather than delivery date management. If you look at the expediting function which consists of four major categories.

1. Coordination
2. Monitoring
3. Assuring
4. Reporting.

Coordination and monitoring are the major functions of expediting whereas assurance end reporting is the resulted output of both. In some cases, the documentation of the above four categories are widely overlooked. Ignored, but monitoring, Assurance, and reporting this parameter are the key indicator for supplier performance monitoring and evaluation. An Expeditor's job is more important where he/she has to work with multidisciplinary professionals regularly to monitor and prevent unwanted conflict and issues.

An expeditor is directly involved with the supplier in the field/behind the desk, where inputs from the expeditor's collected data, help the supplier performance evaluation process which can be performed later by another fellow professional. Supplier performance monitoring is preferred where a new assignment of new collaboration way of business is expected. Supplier performance monitoring and evaluation are often applied as a selective process before the order finalization where a high probability of timely service is calculated on facts collected and analyzed during the process. Hence supplier performance monitoring is not just a process of monitoring but is a business tool which is helping in achieving desired goals.

That is why an expeditor is a best and fit choice for the procurement whereas an internal employee (expeditor) can monitor the process closely and impartial facts are recorded. There is various metric of supplier performance monitoring which can be very in every organization but major performance monitoring metrics are followed as:

1. Quantity verification order Vs actual
2. Advance shipping notice Vs proof of delivery
3. On-time delivery performance
4. Ordered value Vs invoiced value
5. Inspection of planned unit Vs balance for inspection units
6. Lead time variance
7. Gap analysis
8. Comparison with other suppliers
9. Organization defined monitoring metrics

Supplier performance monitoring is a more complex process as it is fact-based and the expeditor is a part of the process.

1. Quantity verification order Vs actual

This performance monitoring is a very basic method where no stringent quality standards are defined and measurement of supplier performance is primarily focused on quantifiable achievements. Since an expeditor is in the vendor/supplier's place these performance criteria can be closely monitored and measured periodically. As an expeditor has access to vendor/supplier orders details and other required quality criteria and documents while doing an expediting supplier performance can be measured in plain sight without any additional interference at vendor/supplier's place.

This method of supplier measurement and monitoring is applied before awarding a long-term contract or an order with sizeable quality to assure delivery promptly.

This method is used for bulk items, other materials which are similar where production or manufacturing comes with repetitive orders from the same buyer/client. Where both parties will agree on contractual terms. The role of the expeditor is important in this method as he/she is doing the expediting and maintaining demands of procurement, as he /she constantly monitoring the progress of the orders, keeping the progress periodically, which are important inputs, tools for performance monitoring which can be helpful for vendor/supplier performance evaluation.

Definition of Quantity verification is different in each organization. Some organizations rely on vendor/supplier notification/information for the readiness of materials, some organizations prefer verified Quantity after inspection and physical delivery at their premises, henceforth this method is a very basic calculative method of many.

Supplier Details			Quality Received					Delivery Rating %
ABC Corporation	Order Qty Units	Delivery Date Ex Works	18/02/	18/03	18/04	20/5	Balance Qty	
Order-1386	10000	18-02-2001	10000				0	100
Order-1387	20000	18-03-2001		20000			0	100
Order-1388	8000	18-04-2001			7500		500	93.75
Order 1389	14000	20-5-2001				14000	0	100
Overall Delivery Success Percentage								98.43

This is an example of this method where all facts are recorded and used in Performance Rating.

2. Advance shipping notice Vs proof of delivery

In Supplier Performance Monitoring, another very popular metric is Advance shipping notice is verified by proof of delivery. Advance shipping notice (ASN) is a notification of pending deliveries, similar to a packing list. It is usually sent in an electronic format. As in the Final Outcome of expediting efforts advance shipping note shows completion of expediting activities but it also adds the credential to the information provided by an expeditor. Advance shipping notice is provided by the supplier as a part of the orders delivery agreement. As an expeditor, he/she is been involved in final delivery efforts, where he/she witness the manufacturing processes and finally comes to resulting in delivery, where expediting the delivery is part of the process and advance shipping notice is one of the supplier performance metric, where an expeditor is part of the SPM process.

The ASN is an important trend in the trade where both buyer and supplier use modern technologies to serve the final goal. As in the example, the Shipment will be sent by sea on 20 TEU Containers, with the itemized packing list in advance, although it provides information similar to the Bill of lading, its function is very different. While the Bill of lading is meant to accompany a load on its path, the goal of the ASN is to provide information to the destination's receiving operations well in advance of delivery. Where the buyer will verify the shipment as received at the designated destination as declared by the supplier. In the whole process expeditor's involvement may not seem very important but as in a part of the buyer's team, an expeditor has to do everything to achieve the final goal of delivery.

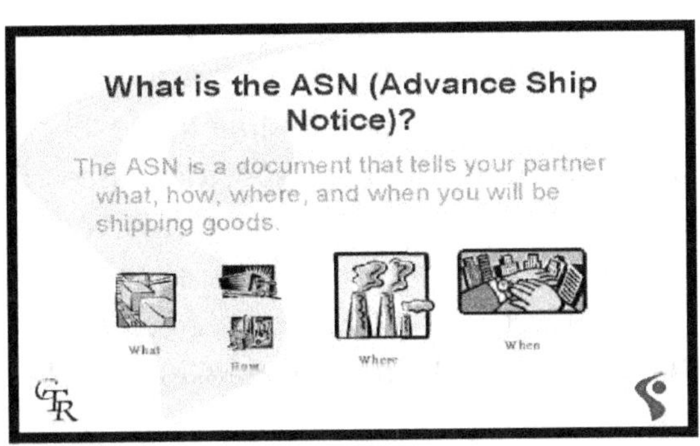

3. On-Time Delivery performance

On-Time Delivery refers to a key performance indicator measuring the rate of finished product and deliveries made in time. This rate is expressed in the total number of units delivered within a set period defined by the customer and the supplier.

In Today's fast-growing industries many organizations use the adaptive methodology to save cost, space, and employee engagement, to achieve this parameter, organizations used an on-time delivery method where an organization procurement team directly stays upfront for any delivery-related constraints. On-time delivery is most crucial for an organization. An Expeditor involvement in the process may be more important where on-time delivery of goods is shown concerned. In-process procurement uses an expeditor's involvement to maintain the performance of the supplier to support the final delivery of the product. An expeditor / has to be dealt with by the supplier where performance is critically compromised and he/she has to closely work with the supplier. On-time delivery performance is mostly achieved with some efforts of expediting involvement. Hence this is the most stressful metric where expeditor has to be given the extra effort and sometimes exceptional thinking can serve the outcome. As in example. A Small project of water treatment package involves 02 nos of pumps, which can be used for raw water inlet. Where late delivery of pumps is not a desirable outcome. Hence to maintain the OTD performance expediting is necessary.

The on-time Delivery term is often used as Delivery schedule adherence as per organization definition. As per Expediting point of view, the whole expediting process and expeditor involvement are based on maintaining on-time delivery performance from the beginning or in between, that's why there is a very important metric of supplier performance.

4. **Ordered value Vs invoiced value**

As A part of supplier performance monitoring, one of the metrics of performance measurement is value comparison, as an expeditor, this metric is widely used for package and project items where multiple items are included. This method is mostly used behind the desk rather than on the field. As an expeditor has to verify the order value & Received invoice value, the expeditor also has to verify the scope of supply and needed more information in Received items which is supported by goods Receipt note, Site clearance, quality clearance, and physical delivery proof, which is required analytical approach, it is mostly performed within an organization. This method is often used for desk expediting where progress is measured by various milestones. This metric has commercial aspects and has to be measured with multiple parameters for actual progress.

For example, a package of water treatment plants has invoice conditions, where suppliers have to send material with conditional terms.

M/s Roller Filters	Total order Value	Details Analysis of invoiced values			
Order No: 1489-2001	$1,000,000.00				
Sr No	% based Payment against	% of total value	Order value	Invoiced value	Difference in Values
1	Major Raw Material identification & Acceptance of 2nd party inspection	20	$200,000.00	$180,000.00	$20,000.00
2	Major Equipment Manufactured & inspected Accepted against 2nd party inspection	15	$150,000.00	$160,000.00	-$10,000.00
3	Pipeline, membrane, skid and panel inspected against 2nd party inspection and dispatched	10	$100,000.00	$110,000.00	-$10,000.00
4	Electrical and instrument panel manufactured and inspection against 2nd party inspection and dispatched	15	$150,000.00	$150,000.00	$0.00

5	Major Equipment installation at site with 2nd party inspection witnessed and cleared by site personal for operation	20	$200,000.00	$200,000.00	$0.00
6	Rest of all project material installation and testing at site with parameters acceptance by 2nd party inspection & site personal	10	$100,000.00	$100,000.00	$0.00
7	All spares inspection and acceptance at site personal with 2nd party inspection	10	$100,000.00	$100,000.00	$0.00
	Total Value		$1,000,000.00	$1,000,000.00	$0.00

Ordered value vs invoiced value has to be reviewed as per the claim by the supplier and analyzed before the final decision. An expeditor can verify the claims better as he/she has full access to orders and other information. Hence Expediting is not limited by delivery warnings but has to offer a more diverse management approach towards the organization.

5. **Inspection of planned unit Vs balance for inspection units.**

This method is used for performance monitoring where the buyer has provided inspection resources generally an agency or inspection Personnel from the buyer's organization. In situations, the performance is only measured by inspection acceptance criteria, where the supplier has to offer inspection of the planned unit as per the Delivery dates and inspection has to verify with quality standards and also nos have to be verified against claims of the supplier. Most commonly this practice is used for bulk items or items that are similarly divided by physical appearance, application in use, where inspection has to be done before dispatching the material. Since an expeditor is in the field, he/she can monitor the progress and can be back traced if the progress of the planned unit falls short in the inspection procedure. As an expeditor, he/she must have to ensure the progress of planned activities must be performed as per the schedule.

6. Lead time variance

A lead time is a latency between the initiation and completion of a process. For example, the lead time between the placement of an order and delivery of the product by a given manufacturer might be 2 weeks to 04 weeks, depending on various particularities.

A general definition of "manufacturing lead time" is the total time required to manufacture an item, including order preparation time, queue time, setup time, run time, move time, inspection time, and put-away time. For make-to-order products, it is the time between the release of an order and the production and shipment that fulfill that order. For make-to-stock products, it is the time taken from the release of an order to production and receipt into finished goods inventory.

For example, A Small Water treatment project lead time is given by supplier A is 05 weeks and supplier B has given a lead time of 04 weeks. Where variance of 01 weeks between suppliers does not seem very much but when the client required the project delivery in 03 weeks then lead time variance had to be monitored and expedited for exploration of better options.

An expeditor's job is more important where the lead time is shortened than proposed/actual. Or in particular, cases when lead time is extended than defined. An expeditor's assignment is more vigilant when he/she reviews all the scenarios where lead time can be reduced to achieve delivery. In some cases, an expeditor has to compare lead time with other suppliers to find out to improvise and also to find reasons for the delay.

For example, Mutt stage filtering pressure vessels system where quality assurance plan has mandatory requirements of raw materials physical and chemical check testing.

Where Supplier A has a house testing laboratory facility where the 01-week time of awaiting testing sample's results can be utilized in other manufacturing operations.

Where Supplier B has to depend on the outside the laboratory for raw material's physical and chemical check testing.

With ref to supplier performance supplier A has a better advantage over manufacturing time, an expeditor has to measure and assess performance on capability, facility, and other factors.

Supplier Performance is a part of Expediting and expeditor is a fit choice for doing the same.

7. GAP Analysis

Gap analysis is defined as a method of assessing the differences between the actual performance and expected performance in an organization or the Assignment.

The GAP is Defined by the space between Required Performance and Actual performance, in expediting an expeditor is constantly doing performance analysis and measurement of Requirement Vs Actual, where he/she can identify the Reason for GAP Between Actual and requirement were multiple factors of Assessment like Manpower, Quality, Time, Cost, capability, Facility, logistic, sub-vendor Assessment, the performance of individual and team, are involved.

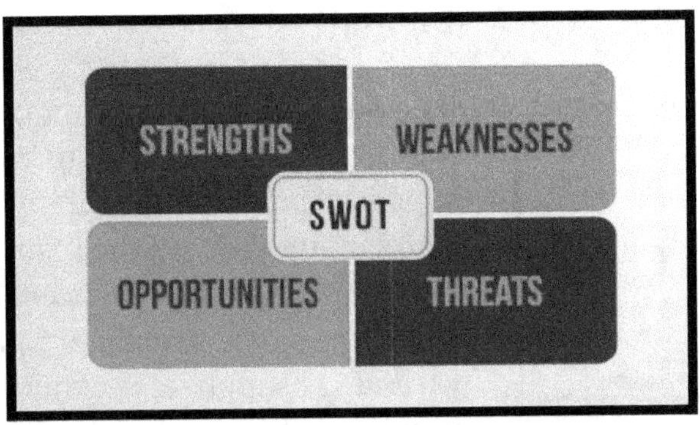

The most Practicing method in GAP Analysis is the SWOT method, SWOT is defined by Strengths, weaknesses, opportunities, threats.

In Expediting an expeditor may or may not be following the same methodology without knowing that he/she is doing a part performance analysis on a routine basis. An expeditor has to focus on his/her particular Assignments for achieving results, in the due process he/she may have to SWOT analysis on supplier's entire infrastructure.

In General terms, An Expeditor does SWOT Analysis frequently, which is part of the expediting, Where An expeditor has to Review the Supplier's Strengths for performing an assignment, Weaknesses for delay prevention, Opportunities for progress/ improvement,

Threats analysis for known, unknown reasons. (Threat Analysis is performed in Extreme Conditions where the loss of revenue, loss of business, loss of Reputation, Competition domination) Threats analysis, may not be Relevant to an expeditor, but as in part of the procurement team, some threats are very real and need to be assessed and terminated on high priority.

8. Comparison with Other suppliers

In supplier performance monitoring, the most practical way to measure supplier performance is to do a comparison with other suppliers, when an organization needs to do supplier performance among various suppliers, the most promising supplier's performance is considered as a benchmark and it will become measurement parameters among other suppliers. In comparison, the top-performing supplier has established the highest satisfaction criteria which have to be explained, implied, and Followed at other suppliers' places and keeping performance monitored until solid improvement starts to show in results. In particular, an expeditor has to be assigned for comparative analysis with other suppliers' performance data to step up the performance of the targeted supplier. This practice is mainly popular with Supply chain management, where knowledge sharing is preferred for better results towards organizational excellence.

9. Organization defined supplier performance monitoring system.

An Organization is driven by best management practices, steady financial progress, and most importantly by the organization's people. Who can establish their criteria of supplier performance, as per needs of the business and can establish a healthy relationship with the supplier in a long way, As in today's trends suppliers are considered as growth partners, as this step creates a linear relationship between organization and supplier, where traditional top to a bottom relationship is not considered? Organization-defined performance monitoring systems may be developed with higher standards of performance to match with the organization's performance in the market. Henceforth an individual needs to understand the organization's Definition and has to act accordingly.

For above Method or Metrics are the measurement tools for supplier performance that are utilized in Field for the practice by an expeditor regularly. Henceforth an expediting is an Elaborated and complex process of progress assurance and delivery satisfaction.

An expeditor must have to skills of supplier performance monitoring, which later can be evolved into supplier performance evaluation, both skills are beneficial at individual levels and organization level as well because a skilled expeditor is considered as eyes and ears on the field, where rest of the organization may not have privileged enough to deal with suppliers directly with a business perspective. Now all my readers can understand that expediting is now more than a late delivery warning. It is more of an improvised assurance approach towards the final goal of delivery. Hence expediting is not an easy job or just a job.

Conclusion: Supplier performance assurance is the fundamental duty of an expeditor and needs to be focused on it.

***

Chapter -7: Onsite Reporting, and records management

In this Chapter we will be discussing Reporting and Records management, as expediting efforts are not established till proper reporting through the end-user is established. As in the popular concept of paper works where "no job is finished until pater work is done". In expediting pater work is also important but reporting and records management is part of expediting's 04 major functions.

1) Coordination
2) Monitoring
3) Assuring
4) Reporting.

Nowadays In expediting Reporting is evolved through just paperwork, in practice various organizations use systems. Like, SAP, ERP, MS Project, Primavera, and other various real-time tracking systems, in that system a user, an expeditor has access to the system on the field and after verification of all progress & progress, expeditor can update the milestone, key process indicators, on real-time through the system, hence more transparency more efforts are expected from an expeditor. System-based Progress updates, milestones, Key process Indicator's update, critical path tracking, are useful tools and techniques for forecasting further planning, and with the perspective of project management reporting is considered as a part of schedule management. Hence Reporting is very important in the process.

Report is categorized as: (Every organization has its Method of Reporting)

1) Daily Flash Report
2) Periodic Progress Report
3) Surprise visit Report
4) Preventive corrective actions report.
5) Inspection Report / certificate.

These reports are generated on-site and circulated within the pre-defined audience. Some reports are prepared offsite where further deep analytical review is needed before conclusion and circulation.

Daily Flash Report

Daily flash Report is a very basic and minimal Report which is used for major progress reporting, where all other details are not necessarily required. As an example, a manufacturing Schedule consists of 08 Different Activities with a period of 01 weeks. Each day visiting expeditor makes sure that activity is performed under his/her supervision and by end of the day he/she prepares the report and gets it signed by the supplier and sent it to his/her reporting manager. A daily Flash Report is verification of planned activity as per forecast or schedule plan. Daily Flash Report Contains minimum Details like purchase order No, Annual contact No, item Details, Qty, Progress updates plan vs actual, etc. as Mentioned earlier Daily Flash Report required fewer efforts and is used for verification of planned activities. The organization uses various templates as per their needs, but the purpose of the report is for a progress update, plan vs actual, and verification of planned activities. It's also being used for external agencies based on expediting, where expediting tenure is more than a day and procurement wants updates of progress daily till completion of the assignment. Now all can understand the importance of the report and why it is needed.

Periodic Progress Report

A periodic Progress Report is required where more complex operations are performed and progress is only verified after a certain amount of monitoring through an expeditor, inspector, and other Representative of the organization. A periodic Progress report is prepared with milestones and key process indicators, and other defined parameters, which are part of planning management, schedule management. This report is prepared on a weekly, fortnight, monthly basis, due to large complex operations are performed where the supplier has to coordinate other resources, agencies, internal engineering department, quality department, where everyone has functional responsibilities and all activities have a successor and predecessor activities, without performing them, progress and process cannot go forward, as in the example, A pressure vessel manufacturing only starts when raw material is identified and inspected, tested through 2nd party inspection from buyer side, without it manufacturing cannot be started, similarly manufacturing cannot be started until raw material acceptance is done as per quality assurance plan which is signed by both parties. In this scenario, a daily progress report does not add qualitative values to reporting, instated an expeditor can invest his efforts in coordination with the manufacturer, inspection agency for completion of planned activities, and he/she can report the progress of the entire gamut of activities performed through the week, a fortnight, which can be helpful to measure milestone, key process indicators for planned vs actual measurement.

A periodic progress report is a surety document, which measures both the performance of the supplier and an expeditor.

Surprise visit report.

In the Business where priorities are less addressed or ignored, a surprise visit to the supplier end gives a clear picture of performance drop. Nowadays in capitalism's era, everyone has their own business needs to follow, where priority and targets are changed rapidly and focus shifts easily from one client to another. A Surprise visit mat reveals reasons for the delay, loss of attention, and communication ignorance. In situations like this, documented findings help assess the situation.

A real case study of Surprise Visit can reveal real reasons for inadequate supplier performance.

As an Expeditor, Mr. Z Has Assigned to investigate the delay of Supplier M/s ABC Filters, where a Small water treatment project is delayed by 02 weeks, after sending several Reminders and phone calls, the supplier didn't respond for progress updates. After failing on communication an expeditor had visited the supplier's place unannounced. After several discussions with the Manufacturing head, plant manager, General Manager, and several authorities. After spending a fair amount of time, the owner of the company agreed to meet the expeditor, and upon meeting the owner revealed that the company's other partner has sold his share to another investor and the current partner has creative differences about manufacturing practices, financial wellness, infrastructure, and current manpower. The New investor has asked to change infrastructure and cost-cutting initiatives, which are not relevant in the supplier's original partner's point of view when the company's financial structure is solid and the business is profiting. A new investor has gone with a legal way of new policy implication and in the process, all other functions are affected. The supplier has managed the new investor's initiatives and keeps the company running with minimal changes for new management policies. The supplier has assured that in the due process delay of 02 weeks will be covered up with extra time, additional resources, allocation in manufacturing.

Now Mr. Z has gone to great lengths of communication for getting answers, and finally, he has got the result. Now Mr. Z has Prepared a Surprise visit Report and circulated it to the concerned authorities, where his efforts are appreciated and acknowledged for clearing the haze.

Preventive/corrective actions report.

Preventive and corrective actions Reports are needed when due to the very demanding nature of business, An Expeditor has to take preventive actions when planned activities deviate. Also, an expeditor has to take corrective actions when planned activities are not performed on time and delay is occurred, in both scenarios, an expeditor has to report both actions when more transparency in the act is a necessity of the trade.

As in Practice, an expeditor has seen a delay of 02 weeks due to inadequate manpower allocated for his assignment. He reports it in his records and discusses the supplier with evidence. The supplier agreed to add sufficient manpower for the assignment. As in practice when in any scenario, finding, observation, the deviation is materializing in some sort of Record, it creates a psychological advancement for arguments and discussion. It also helps the originator to exercise his/her ownership and dominance of the assignment.

Inspection Report / certificate.

Inspection Report or inspection Certificates is documented evidence of process competition, but acceptance depends on when inspection reports /certificates indicate no deviation or observation for quality assurance. Inspection Report/certificates show the compilation and acceptance of assignments. In general inspection reports/certificates are issued by inspection and quality personnel from the buyer side or an external agency is nominated. An expeditor also can issue an Inspection Report/certificate as per directives from procurement. Inspection is part of the milestone when assignments reach for final delivery and it is also a part of expediting procedure and needs to be monitored. In some cases, an expeditor has to coordinate with quality personal/external agencies for performing an inspection on site. Henceforth reporting is not just paperwork but it has a sizable impact on assignments and needs to be generated with a cautious approach.

In addition, an expeditor has to interpret data correctly as some suppliers are using their system for progress updates and tracking. Where supplier's definition of completion of activities is differently defined, other than procurement definition of completion. Henceforth an expeditor has to review data thoroughly to prevent conflicts.

Records management

Record Management is a part of knowledge management, where data is processed it takes a form of information when information is materialized under various categories it becomes a Record.

As An expeditor starts expediting with required data like purchase order, contract copy, technical documents, it is data required starting an expediting, when expeditor process this data for progress, process identification, measurement of Deliverables, it becomes information that can be materialized in some sort of formats, then keeping this information under vendor performance category it becomes a record. Hence Record management is an evident knowledge-sharing process of an organization. Record Management is useful for review and reference of supplier performance, delivery constraints and resolution, lessons learned, evaluation, cost, and other metrics.

Record Management is also instrumental for transparency and effectiveness, accountability. An expeditor is using various information for analysis of supplier performance, assignments progress, process evaluation, commercial aspects, it all has to be materialized for evolutionary and educational purposes. It may sound strange but an expeditor's job is more just to expedite delivery dates. Nowadays organizations are more focused on knowledge sharing, information, and Record management. They follow standardized or defined ways of Record management, which can be useful for future reference and learning purposes.

There are various types of Records as per organization structure.

Correspondence records.
Accounting records.
Legal records.
Personnel records.
Progress records
Miscellaneous records. & others

Progress record is the most relevant type of record management for an expeditor, from expediting point of view Record management is the supervision and administration of digital or paper records, regardless of format.

***

Chapter – 8: Desk Expediting

Desk Expediting is nowadays a popular concept in procurement, where unlike the field expediting this kind of service is generally performed on low criticality or non-strategic supplies. Desk expediting provides a valuable tool for monitoring the progress orders with a manufacturer. Working behind the desk in the expediting gives more indirect communication, interpretation of supplier and organization's metrics and data.

Desk expediting is best used to obtain general information like submission of the required documentation, placement of suborders, overall progress of the fabrication manufacturing, and deliveries; relevant to a certain supply. This kind of service is generally performed at specific milestones or according to a frequency established by the customers, or suggested by the expeditor. The success of the desk expediting service is maximized if performed in conjunction with field expediting visits.

In desk expediting supplier, Contact is established before the introduction and milestone, deliverables of orders are pre-defined, preset for measurement and desk expeditor has to perform an expediting from behind desk through the phone using, organization system, templates, the information provided. Desk expediting consists of verification of milestone completion, with adequate evidence provided by the supplier, external agency & others. Desk Expediting begins with supplier orders details, information which is provided by procurement. Desk expediting involves written communication & waterworks, like, Emails, physical order dispatch, letter of commitment, invoices, internal/external agencies contracts, overseas supplier invoicing, coordination with the site manager, quality documents status, inspection coordination, logistic coordination, dispatch verification, and other various responsibilities.

Desk expediting most cases involving a milestone basis expediting, supplier order confirmation, Assignments starts with Raw material procurement verification, manufacturing forecast, inspection dates forecast, dispatch date forecast, invoicing forecast, supplier invoicing verification, payments clearance on actual completion, payments tracking, and other.

Desk expeditor's major Responsibilities are followed as:
1) Supplier order confirmation
2) Order Progress updates/ periodically progress Report circulation.
3) Planned vs actual comparison.
4) Internal customer management.
5) High priority items tracking and reporting.
6) Invoicing and contracts management.
7) Internal /external coordination

Desk Expediting starts with order confirmation from the supplier, supplier planned schedule for the milestone, internal agencies coordination, internal project team, procurement team's Requirements of material, setting properties of highly required item, and has to inform supplier from the desk and getting a positive reply from supplier, if not received a positive reply than the loss of debating conference call and communication has to be made from behind the desk, which is not quite an easy job.

Supplier order confirmation & order progress updates.

In a daily routine e of desk expediting, an expeditor has to work with no of supplier for daily tracking order confirmation raw materials procurement verification, manufacturing status of existing orders, material movement, planned s actual deliverable measurement and analysis, where milestone forecast is received from supplier desk expeditor has to review with master order data and then have to circulate internally, an experienced expeditor will very quickly assess whether the order is progressing consistent with the plan or whether alternative measures are needed to verify and presumably improve the order progress. In the whole process, an expeditor has to circulate progress update reports periodically which can be done after the careful analysis of facts and figures.

Planned vs actual comparison.

In desk expediting an expeditor has to get a scheduled plan for every order and line item wise. After receiving a scheduled plan an expeditor has to review for deviation, after comparison deviation in schedule has to escalate to the supplier and get in line with milestone requirement. In some cases, desk expeditors have to send another field expeditor for the resolution of delayed items. Daily planned vs actual comparison is a necessity of the desk expediting.

Internal customer management.

Since an expeditor is a facilitator between procurement and final user. Often request for information, process update, schedule changes, supplier meeting arrangement, priority changes, etc. since an expeditor knows the assignments, he/she can use his/her sense of wisdom to serve better.

High priority items tracking and reporting.

As in assignments behind the desk, an expeditor is a focal point of the procurement and project team, where the priority of required items is to be handled with a cautious approach since an expeditor is a facilitator between procurement and final user. Often request for information, priority items progress, urgent items follow up, replacement items follow up, daily progress report, inspection schedule, dispatch scheduling, Goods receipt note, Material Record book, etc. behind the desk an expeditor has to manage all high priority items delivery and has to coordinate with external agencies, transporters which are highly focused and demanding in nature.

Invoicing and contracts management.

Invoicing and contracts management is handled by accounting and procurement in various organizations, but in many other organizations, and expeditor has the authority of preparing invoices, subcontracts preparation, supplier payment approval, and others. Where an expeditor has to check all preparation and double-check before final invoicing hits in the system.

An expeditor has to be prepared for any kind of situational drawback which is generated by anyone within the organization, outside the organization, human error, system constraints, etc.

I am quoting my own experience for a case study where you can understand, as an expeditor, I had to encounter an uncharted situation, in which a solution was not available and had to go to great length for finding a compromising solution.

As in the final steps of invoicing, I was preparing a DRAFT invoice for our client M/s Romtex Pharma, where I have to prepare the same through our ERP system, where I have to fill in necessary details and have to send to the Project Manager for review and approval.

When I have prepared all the details and punch in the system for the draft, the system shows full Package value was not reflected in the Draft invoicing, and the difference of $102,300.00 is shown in the system, I was surprised to see that much deviation and has to discard the draft and prepared again but values Remains the Same for package Qty.

The system Has not calculated the full package value. I have no choice but to stop the process and go for the entire backtracking of project material Data.

I have asked my System Administrator for help & he gave me a look and said "System work people don't" I couldn't understand the quote but I have to ask for a solution and he said the System works just fine, plus ensure your project people have done everything as per SOP.

DRAFT Invoice: ABC-1386-0001-R0			
Client: Romtex Pharma Date: 01-4-2010			
Package Qty	Package Value (Material Master Sheet)	Actual Package Qty	Actual Value
1	$10,230,000	0.99	$10,127,700.00
		Difference in Values to invoice 100%	$102,300.00

I have no choice but to investigate the same, I have pulled out all master material data which has 2032 no's individual items, pulled our actual material goods receipt data, and have to compare both with spreadsheet functions. Surprisingly, I have found that a Small compressor unit was not issued on the shop floor and it was not received at Store from the supplier. I have an inquiry about the issued compressor unit and it revealed that the compressor unit was originally bought for another project under a different business unit, project personal made a deal with another business unit to use their compressor unit because it was similar in size and specification, our project agreed to give our compressor unit to them upon arrival. But in the whole process, no documentation of stock transfer was done, no internal invoicing has been done, neither compressor unit was restocked from listing and issued to our project as per stock transfer protocol. And in the whole process invoicing was delayed by 02 days to complete the formalities. In this whole situation finally, an expeditor has found the discrepancies until the system hits the final step and the true nature of ignorance has been revealed. In this kind of situation, an expeditor has to apply a cautious and investigative approach to reach the final goal of service with higher operating standards.

Contracts Management

A contract is a document that details the products being sold, sets the agreed-upon prices, and defines the terms and conditions of the purchase agreement for a certain period. Contracts also provide the value and number of purchase orders and invoices. In desk expediting an expeditor mostly works with contacts as in similar, identical, iterative, nature items are manufactured and supplied under various purchase orders but under single or multiple contracts. Which has to be followed and reviewed by an expeditor

Contracts Management does not entirely depend upon an expeditor, but when a contract is established between procurement and seller. An Expeditor is the instrument of execution that manages the process of managing contracts, deliverables, deadlines, contract terms, and conditions while ensuring customer satisfaction. An expeditor is an essential factor to execute a contract within the time as he/she is witnessing and controlling post-contract activities with responsibility and authority invested by the higher management of the organization.

In Expediting Contract Management Knowing what to expect at each of the four essential stages of the process will increase the supplier's ability to meet contract requirements and deliver optimal results.

1) Planning stage
2) Monitoring stage
3) Execution stage
4) Delivery stage

Planning stage

In contracts Management, planning stages may involve a preliminary document known as a "letter of intent" which is a document declaring the preliminary commitment of one party to do business with another. Most of the organization starts the work after the contract is signed by both parties and all the details have been discussed and recorded, meanwhile, some organization works on mutual trust and the seller starts the work when only a "letter of intent" is issued and the final contract balances, as they know each other needs very well and this kind of trust comes with long term strategic partnership. Henceforth an expeditor may have to work with minimal Documents to start the expediting and has worked closely with procurements and multi-discipline like internal engineering, Quality Department, Site Management, Accounts, where work has been started and key reference documents like engineering drawings, quality manuals, procedures, are due in process for approval. In this situation, an expeditor's role is expanded beyond supplier engagement and internal departmental coordination starts which needs extra effort and time. In planning when a contract is due for approval an expeditor has to do partial planning of work in progress, by defining early stages of deliverables, and key process indicators on his own. So when processes are due for approval, revision, and implementation, an expeditor's duty never stops until everything comes under the right order. In other words, an expeditor has to take care of business before it starts contractually.

Monitoring stage

In Contracts Management. After the planning stage, a most important stage comes, which ensures timely execution of planned activities, is the monitoring stage, in which under a single contract, multiple orders, various items fall under the responsibility of the desk expeditor.

Large EPC and other construction organizations use desk expediting as a monitoring tool, as procurements of multiple items, which are different, needs attention and tracking closely, in that scenario field expediting on a routine basis is not a preferred choice, where the desk expediting fits the GAP between the flow of information from Supplier to procurement/project.

In desk expediting monitoring is done evidently with supplier's schedule vs actual work, material inspected vs material dispatched, work in progress, Material Management, internal /external Agencies reporting verification, Proof of Delivery, Site Report, Goods Receipt note Etc., Desk Expediting often called as telephone expediting, but there is a distinct difference in operating, as desk expediting involves, multiple communication, like Email, phone, audio-video Conferences, system-generated Reports, etc., while telephone expediting involves, very less milestone which can easily verifiable over the phone and can take preventive corrective actions, while in desk expediting, an expeditor has to rely on multiple sources for progress updates.

In Desk Expediting due to the nature of high value and high no of items, a group of Expeditors can be assigned with a functional manager for desired results achievement.

For monitoring purposes an expeditor has to work with a project management group, closely for progress updates, as large EPC & other construction businesses work on phase-wise planning like OBSL, ISBL, underground, aboveground CAPEX, open, and other defined phases are used.

Where OSBL outside Battery Limits (OSBL) is defined as utilities, common facilities, and other equipment and components not included in the ISBL definition. OSBL refers to systems (equipment pieces and associated components) that support several units. Typical OSBL equipment includes cooling towers, water treatment facilities, tanks farms, etc.

Inside Battery Limits (ISBL) are defined as all equipment and associated components (piping, etc.) that act upon the primary feed stream of a process. ISBL is functional-based and refers to equipment and other components that are solely dedicated to a single process whether or not the equipment is physically located within the geographical boundaries of the unit.

In monitoring stages expeditors have to go for comparison and analytical approach for maximizing the work by using the continuous expeditious approach, in which room for error is very marginal and almost none. In reality when progress is behind the schedule, or critical desk expediting is supported with field visits to get desired results, desk expediting shows evidence of supplier delay and field visitors can ask for the reason to investigate and correct the delaying reasons. Also in monitoring the stage desk expeditor has to make priority plans as per the needs of the project and construction. Priority plan involves pushing up the needed items ahead of the production schedule, changes of the production schedule, assigning of other/additional resources (inclined with supplier discussion). Dispatch movement assurance, site Receipt tracking, etc. Performing this kind of continuous corrective approach is recognized by industry and Expeditor is called AS "MASTER SCHEDULERS" for their dynamic and adaptive functionalities.

Execution stage

Contract management execution is the assuring stage in which planned activities form a final product. Execution is only accepted when it is done properly, within quality standards, and endorsed by quality personnel. This is the basic definition of execution in expediting & contract management. A contract may be listed with quality standards and requirements. With expediting perspective an execution is a milestone completion, not full progress. Execution may be consistent with most important activities execution is a predecessor activity of delivery. The Execution phase involves carrying most of the required details of the assignments to deliver the final product to the customer. An execution involves Major Responsibilities like

1) People Management
2) Information distribution

People Management

In execution, people are defined as not just supplier's people, but whole beneficiaries of the process are recognized as people, Aka, Supplier, Procurement, and customer are the key people. People management in execution is the entire gamut of activities known as, Assigning & assessing Responsibilities of supplier's network, priority management, corrective actions, which lead to the execution. People management required straight and effective communication. For example after final testing multiple filter vessels, it must be moved for the next operation of protective coating, when testing in charge has not filled the work datasheet and cleared for protective coating. The next person cannot move for operation without proper documentation, in this scenario a small overlooked process shows no harm no foul, but in reality, the next guy does not move the operation and starts another job, and a delay of 12 hours is added when almost all critical activities are completed. In addition to the situation, a client representative comes the next day for the progress updates, and nobody can answer the reason for the delay. If the clear instruction to the people has circulated correctly, then this whole situation can be avoided, henceforth people management is the important exception.

Information distribution

In the earlier Segment, we have focused on people management, now information distribution is the next part of the execution process. The information distribution is divided into two segments

1) Prior execution instructive information
2) After execution indicative information

Prior execution instructive information

This kind of information generally arrives after the conclusion of setting a parameter, a milestone, and a key process indicator, which needs to be carried out as planned or early as needed. This defined information clearly states the instructions to move things as planned or in the course of correction or move things ahead of the existing line. This information needs to be prioritized, acknowledged, and distributed to the performers. Prior execution instruction information is by default in nature. Hence the expeditors have to circulate this information to all notified parties. In desk expediting this kind of information is categorized as an urgent list, Priority list, constraint items requirement, SOS list, etc. As the desk expeditor, the reasonability and responsibilities are crucial for the assignment. As in Example: 100 cartridge filters are planned for dispatch in the 3rd week, all notified parties agreed to the delivery in the 3rd week at designated place-A. But after the 2nd-week new instructive information comes that 30 out of 100 Filters are to be shipped in separate packages at different locations place-B. Just before 01 weeks the instructive information comes and needs to be circulated with an updated shipping address.

After execution indicative information

As in the name, it defines the after execution, a parameter, a milestone, a key process indicator, which needs to be carried out as planned or early as needed is done rightfully, and this information needs to be circulated. A medium Circulation of information is multiple, An Email, A updated spare sheet, a milestone update in the system, MS Project, SAP, other systems updates which show real-time updates to the end-user. As in the example, process Receipt in the ERP system is directly reflected in the procurement dashboard, which helps the procurement/project to track the item. Another Example is after inspection and certification items are ready for dispatch, a Shipment control number is generated for the cleared items, but the cleared items remain ideal at the supplier's place until another batch is ready for inspection and certification which can be sent in the whole package, not partially. But the indication of completed items gives clear accountability and transparency towards the benefits of complete utilization. Of information.

This Elaboration is required because in desk expediting an expeditor has to work with loss of information which needs to be processed independently, accurately, and at the same time he/she to make sure that processed information flows perfectly from Bottom to top hierarchy. In addition, this explanation is more important as some organizations preferred Desk expediting only, where the help of field visit, field expeditor is almost slim to zero or none.

Delivery Stage

In Desk expediting Delivery, it is an individualistic monitoring stage supported for verification by various methods. As in after execution the whole process is not completed until physical delivery of items is initiated. In other words, the Delivery stage is the successor stage of execution. After execution and information distribution a sense of comfort is developing in procurement and supplier's teammates, and they may knowingly unknowingly neglect the delivery assurance efforts, as the delivery preparation is performed by another team, the execution team clears their duties and left the preparation of the whole items for another team, where the high chances of the communication GAP are expected.

Delivery Stage has important steps as;

1)   Preparation

Preparing for delivery of the items is Essential, where packaging, additional reinforcements, protective layering, Sty Check, Containers booking, preparation for transportation, invoicing, shipping manifest, and other criteria needs to be checked, approved, and to be maintained. This all process is time-consuming and needs to be expedited as per the urgency of the business and not to be ignored. In the desk expediting the waiting period between execution and delivery stage has to be monitored with a cautious approach to preventing a further delay. As delay after execution can undo the entire expediting efforts.

2)   Perform Contractual terms.

To perform Contractual terms: As In delivery contractual terms need to be traded carefully, as in some contracts special terms are addressed. As in example 40 % advance payment is required after shipping a manifest submission. In this term, extra coordination and efforts are required. The desk expeditor has to review and act upon it. To manage the delivery, an incoterm (International commercial terms) is Standardized which can be used internationally and domestically.

Internal/External Coordination

In desk Expediting, procurement, supplier, sub-supplier, vendor, inspection agency, Quality Department, business representatives, higher management, another concerned party are involved for business purposes. A desk expeditor is the focal point of communication. To corporate with all, requires great coordination and effective communication. For the ease of operation coordination efforts have to be categorized, acknowledged, and prioritized for higher effective engagement.

Internal coordination: On the desk expediting internal coordination is required when a request for information and actions comes from inside the organization. This required information/instruction can be in any form of progress updates of items, Order Finalization, kick-off meeting, periodically review meeting, any interaction with project & procurement, and to act upon this kind of request/instruction falls under the category of internal coordination.

Major Categories of internal coordination are:

1) Order progress updates
2) specific/special requirement management
3) Kick-off meeting for new order/assignment
4) Review Meetings
5) Departmental follow-up

Order progress updates: This is the most common type of internal coordination of desk expediting, as the desk expeditor is the link between procurement and project team, project managers often request/instruct progress updates of orders on a routine basis. An expeditor maintains constant monitoring and communications with suppliers, and updated information can be available with the expeditor only and he/she has to share the information. In the field expediting the flow of information takes a time to reach its requester. In contrast, the desk expediting the requestor can come to visit the expeditor personally on his/her desk.

Specific/special requirement management: begins the desk expediting specific, special requirement comes from any direction due to urgency of nature. Likewise, a Small water treatment project's expected delivery is in the 4th week but the requester demands to fulfill the delivery in the 3rd week due to the revised fabrication plant at the site. This is a prime example of a specific/special requirement that has to be processed, acknowledged, prioritized, monitored, and to be executed closely.

Kick-off meeting for new order/assignment: Most projected organizations understand the importance of expediting and they include and introduce expediting personnel to the rest of the project team and supplier personnel, to build team spirit. It is also helpful to set clear goals and to understand the hierarchy of the supplier and project team in need of conflicts, escalation, and coordination. It is also helpful to understand the timeline of the project, supplier mode of working, capabilities, capacities, willingness, and others.

A typical Kick-off meeting agenda includes.

1) Introductions
2) Project background
3) Project /assignment purpose
4) Scope
5) Plan
6) Roles
7) Collaboration
8) Questions
9) Next steps

A thoughtfully discussed agenda will leave the team confident about everything from a shared understanding of the vision to the finest details, and it helps to achieve deliverables with lower changes of delay/failure. The desk expediting is a must to be a part of this type of kick-off meeting.

Review Meetings: Review meeting organized for progress updates discussion, new requirements, solutions for existing constraints, plan vs actual progress, backup vs make-up plan discussion, delay analysis, supplier performance, etc. Review meetings are a good communication exchange tool, which is used to address the general and specific issues within the decided timeline. In desk expediting review meeting mostly on basis of progress constraint, delay analysis, alternative solutions, root cause analysis, course of correction, etc. review meeting is the information exchange where the project can discuss details of the current requirements which needs to be updated and completed on priority, on the others side desk expeditor can review the new requirements and act upon it within the planned time frame.

Review Meetings are the center of discussion and it provides exposure to the 360° overview of the project, which is almost invisible from the desk, henceforth review meetings are an essential tool of communication and information exchange. In my point of view as an individual expeditor, he/she must not hesitate to attend such meetings and must have to perform at the front. Review meetings are decisive because at the end of the day people have gathered for the common interest. Where through the presentation of facts, discussion of the current scenario, internal communications, worst-case scenario, and pre-preparation, critical part of the project, financial impacts, and other strategies can be revealed, and it is a painful experience for the expeditor.

The Review meeting has 4 major components.

1) Purpose; the general purpose of the review meeting is to learn from the situation and gain insight into it. It is also helpful to develop the confidence to take better authoritative steps and leadership. The most effective purpose of the review meeting is to get recommendations for required changes.

2) Work outcome: After/during a review meeting any significant changes in the situation in the process can be

improved to get better results. After reviewing team efficiency, operational performance can be improved which is essential to keep the project running as planned.

3) Human outcome: The human outcome in a review meeting may be marginal but it clearly shows commitment towards organization periodic review meetings can produce a sense of collaboration, continuous learning, skill development, which can deepen the connection between the team and the shared mission of the project/organization.

4) Clearing communication GAP: Above all Review meetings are excellent tools for clearing communication GAP between, team, project managers, internal customers, where most of the communication GAP Clears when persons are meeting face to face. With periodic review meetings eventually, people open up their ideas, work progress, team performance, etc., and that later people can act upon with their fine sense of wisdom.

Departmental Follow-up: In the desk expediting departmental follow-up is the main service function of the expeditor. As he/she is the center point for communication requests for itemized updates, urgent items requirements, progress updates, field management, supplier performance review meeting, is the various departmental requested/instructed follow-ups to be answered. Milestone updates, key process indicators completion, and verification did from behind the desk. As most projected organizations are preferred milestone-based tracking, KPI based monitoring, from expeditor which required a great effort in information analysis, interpretation, and presentation, desk expeditor is responsible for coordinating the work of internal departmental follow-up organizing and keeping records, answering phone calls, emails and updating status of the project.

External Coordination: In the desk expediting external coordination is mainly focused on various representatives of vendors, suppliers, external agencies, field expeditors, inspectors, surveyors, logistics personnel 's interaction and communication, etc.

External coordination can be divided into two categories:

1) Vendor/ supplier coordination: vendor. Supplier coordination is the main part of the desk expediting, in reality, information of progress flows from vendor/suppliers to expeditors and then to the procurement. In Desk expediting coordination efforts of expeditors are higher than usual because available tools of communication are phone calls, emails, conferences, information updates in spreadsheet format, system-generated data, etc., As An Expeditor he/she has to coordinate for process/process updates and has to verify the information by supporting evidence.

2) External Agency's coordination: In the desk expediting an expeditor has to rely on information updates from various sources, other than vendor/supplier. In trade, procurement has acquired and authorized multiple agencies, like 2nd/3rd party inspection agencies, external expediting agencies, logistic agencies, to work under contracts. As An expeditor, he/she has to coordinate with such agencies on a requirement basis. For example, An expeditor has to coordinate with inspection agencies to plan inspection of planned units on the 4th week at the supplier's warehouse.

Chapter-9: Logistics Coordination

Logistics refers to the overall process of managing how resources are acquired, stored, and transported to their final destination. In a general business sense logistics is the management of the flow of goods/items between the point of origin and a point of consumption to meet the requirements of customers for organizations. In expediting Logistics coordination /management is a part of the duty of an expeditor or a separate Expeditor can be assigned for the convenience of the requirement of the organization. From expediting point of view, logistics is an assurance of delivery by hiring services of an organization or an individual, Logistic management is a part of supply chain management. Different types of Expediting needs and different approaches for logistics.

Desk Expediting-Logistic Coordination:

In The desk expediting logistic coordination may be a part of expeditor's duty, as most projected organizations have pre-defined delivery terms in their contract where delivery is to be made domestically internationally, inland waterways, by air, etc. In pre-defined terms of delivery expeditor's engagement is limited to check Readiness of shipment, advance shipping notification verification, coordination for delivery preparation, Transporter coordination, delivery documents coordination, overseas delivery assessment, shipping manifest verification as per order, quantity check, packing list verification, site coordination for space management and other aspects.

In a situation when delivery terms are not defined or deliveries in the scope of the buyer where supplier's contractual engagement is limited to manufacturing goods only, where expenses of the logistics are in the scope of the buyer/procurement. In that scenario, an expeditor has to act as a Logistic expeditor as he/ she must have to possess the required knowledge of it. As an occasional logistics expeditor, he/she has to focus on procuring services of the Transporter/agency and has to get approved from procurement in the whole process he /she is responsible to ensure timely and accurate movement of shipment and information. As a desk expeditor, he/she must have led a similar situation to provide excellent customer service as at the end of the day customer satisfaction is on the high priority.

Logistics is categorized into three categories:

Inbound logistics: Inbound logistics coordination is required for goods and items are like raw material which needs to be consumed at the site or preferred location for manufacturing, generally, materials are procured from vendors with minimum quality certification is preferred for inbound logistics. A transporter/ agency will lift the goods/items from the vendor's warehouse, be stored at their facility dispatching as per the planned date. As the desk expeditor, he/ she has to coordinate vendors and transporters for shifting of the goods as per requirement and it will be a part of the desk expeditor's job till good/item is reached site/preferred location for manufacturing. As in the example, The total 30 no's, 12" diameter ERW Pipes, the total length of 12 meters, to shifted from vendor's location to site location and total distance of 170 km have to be recovered from Point A to point B. A vendor has given advance shipping notice that material is ready for shifting as the desk expeditor he/she must have to check with the transporter for specified material shifting and has to give dimension and quantity of material to finalize 40-foot-long open trailer to move the material, in the situation he/she must have to be the mediator between vendor and transporter for the delivery of the goods. And must have to act as temporary Logistic coordinator at the same time.

Outbound logistic: Outbound logistics is defined as when finished products, semi-finished products are moving from production to the next supply chain facility/next processing center. As the desk expeditor he/she must have to verify the finished product readiness, Transport Preparation, documents verification for order fulfillment processes, in outbound logistics expeditor's engagement is coordination basis, as delivery terms are defined in contract and supplier is responsible for delivery of goods, if the delivery terms are not defined and if the delivery is in the scope of procurement and Expeditor has to coordinate with the agency for procuring services and has to act upon it. For example, a small water treatment project is completed and is for shipping. As an expeditor, he/she to verify the shipping documents for the order fulfillment process and has to release for shipping upon successful verification.

Reverse logistic: In supply chain management Reverse logistics refers to the movement of goods/items from customer to manufacture due to concern reasons many reasons of Return of goods/items for example goods/ items in need of servicing, repairs, refurbishing, resale, recycling, recovery, dispose of, upgrade, etc. An expeditor receives notification for such incidents because he/she is the focal point between procurement and customer. Or in such cases, higher management gives such information for processing and resolving through supply chain managers.

For example, A Pressure Vessel has a leakage in the top nozzle and on-site repairing efforts are not allowed due to hazardous conditions and the Pressure Vessel has to send back to the supplier location to investigate, repair, replace. As an expeditor is notified in the process, he/she must have to coordinate with the consumer and transporter for the movement of the goods/items.

Field Expediting-Logistic Coordination:

As a Field expeditor can perform multiple operations including logistics coordination at the supplier's place, warehouse movement of goods for the phase. In the field expediting, the field expeditor performing expediting is an added advantage for an engagement in logistics operation, as in the field an expeditor is known about the predecessor activities of logistics and can easily confirm/verify the preparation of logistics activities. In the field expeditor may have to engage in, inbound logistics, outbound logistics, and sometimes in reverse logistics. As in practice, an expeditor is a person who synchronizes and facilitates the flow of work, material, goods, items against the departmental and the customer requirements.

Logistic coordinator:

In Current business trends most, advanced projected organizations prefer separate logistic coordinators for early/timely delivery of goods. A logistics coordinator works to ensure equipment or supplies arrive on time to the correct customer. As a logistics coordinator has many responsibilities including coordinating with transportation specialists, inspectors, and coordinators. Desk and filed expeditors, supply chain managers, custom clearance agents, international custom law officials, etc. As trade coordination in logistics is huge and time-consuming, henceforth hiring an expert is the smart solution. A logistic coordinator can oversee all supply chain operations, also organizing and managing inventory, storage, and transportation. Analyzing and optimizing logistical procedures. While Reviewing, preparing, and routing purchase orders. A logistic coordinator ensures the safe and timely pick-up and delivery of shipments. Monitoring shipments, costs, timelines, and productivity. Addressing and resolving shipment and inventory issues. Liaising and negotiating with suppliers and retailers. Answering customer queries.

A Logistics Coordinator is preferred for their communication and negotiation skills. They are also well-versed in supply management principles and practices. They have great record-keeping abilities and a customer-oriented approach henceforth in supply chain management logistics coordinator is a key position.

Advancement and improvement in expediting the process

As in supply chain management, project management, engineering procurement & construction, manufacturing business, a need for expediting comes frequently and naturally is fulfilled by fellow expeditors.

As a part of the business an expeditor's discipline must have to evolve from very basic of " late delivery warning" to excellence in a business where from the beginning of the trade an expeditor, supplier, procurement must have to set a common vision for the timely and profitably execution of project/assignment. As to strengthen the relationship between expeditors, suppliers, procurement. A more open and inclusive approach has to be applied. Whereas an expeditor must have to be empowered in decision making in a serious situation. As per my vision, an expeditor will be more efficient if they are steered in the right direction with expert guidance.

An expediter's confidence and sense of ownership can be boosted.

Empowerment: An expeditor must have to be given some sort of empowerment to face the challenges with confidence.

Innovation: As expediting is an iterative process it can be dull/boring sometimes, when an expeditor suggests something innovative it must be acknowledged, processed, and then implemented if it fits in the business profitably. Which can give an expeditor the highest sense of satisfaction.

Appreciation: As expediting is a thankless and iterative process where other than expeditor everybody is thinking is expediting efforts are not worthy of appreciation. Which kills the enthusiasm of an expeditor? Henceforth the famous idiom says " A little appreciation goes the long way" works all the time and proves to be a timeless classic.

Training & education: An update with current product knowledge, manufacturing process knowledge, training in specific areas are the most beneficial steps both for organization and expeditor.

***

FEEDBACK

A small initiative globally for society.

Do you know, a tap that drips once every second wastes about 1,000 litters of water every month?
#SAVE WATER #SAVE EARTH

One Man NGO: Shri Aabid Surati (Painter, Author, Cartoonist, Activist)
www.ddfmumbai.org

We would be happy to have your feedback...☺

Please share your transparent review/feedback/rating to encourage our author or services. Share your testimonials by clicking the link on www.nexus-stories.com

Our books (eBook & Paperback) are available globally.
www.nexus-stories.com # Amazon # Flipkart

@nexus.stories

@nexus_stories

@Nexus Stories

@nexusstories2016

@ nexus-stories

Have a Happy Reading...!!! ☺